WEYERHAEUSER'S FIRST
100 YEARS

TRADITIONS THROUGH THE TREES

Joni Sensel

Documentary Book Publishers

Seattle, Washington

TRADITIONS THROUGH THE TREES
WEYERHAEUSER'S FIRST 100 YEARS

First Edition 1999

Printed in the United States of America

Author: Joni Sensel
Editor: Don Graydon
Contributing Photographers: Gary Darby, Dave Putnam
Photo Editor: Barry Provorse
Copy Editor: Judy Gouldthorpe
Designer: Paul Langland
Weyerhaeuser Editor: Michele Komen
Consulting Historian: Chuck Twining
Managing Editor: Carolyn Margon
Publisher: Barry Provorse

Library of Congress Cataloging-in-Publication Data
LC# 99-32373

Sensel, Joni, 1962 –
Traditions Through the Trees: Weyerhaeuser's First 100 Years / by Joni Sensel
p. cm.
Includes Index
ISBN 0-935503-27-7

1. Weyerhaeuser Company—History. 2. Forest products industry—United States—History. I. Title.

HD9759.W4S46 1999
338.7'63498'0973—dc21

Documentary Book Publishers
615 Second Avenue, Suite 260
Seattle, Washington 98104
(206) 467-4300
e-mail: docbooks@SasquatchBooks.com
www.SasquatchBooks.com

Weyerhaeuser Company
PO Box 2999
Tacoma, Washington 98477-2999
(253) 924-2345
www.weyerhaeuser.com

Printed on Weyerhaeuser Cougar Opaque 80# book paper.

Table of Contents

Foreword

George H. Weyerhaeuser

LOOKING BACK

Our company began 100 years ago with 900,000 acres of timberland, three employees, and a small office in Tacoma, Washington. Our company's namesake—my great-grandfather Frederick Weyerhaeuser—and our original investors were forest industry experts who contributed capital and, perhaps more important, their experience, reputations, and values to the new business.

Weyerhaeuser's values were well ingrained in 1966, the year I became the company's ninth president. They had served our company well for nearly 70 years, because they had been put into practice early in the century and adopted and advanced by succeeding managements. An in-depth look at Weyerhaeuser's values a decade ago produced an affirmation of the key company values that guide us today.

Traditions Through the Trees: Weyerhaeuser's First 100 Years goes a step further. It explores the origins of our values, describes how they influence the company today, and suggests how they will contribute to our future.

During the 50 years that I have been with the company, we have practiced these values and I have observed how they have been applied in our work. I am very proud of the many successes we have achieved, of the milestones we have reached, and of this great company we have created. Weyerhaeuser and our values have stood the test of time—100 years—and I know they will continue to do so. That is why I am dedicating this book to all the people who are Weyerhaeuser: past, present . . . and future.

Sincerely,

George H. Weyerhaeuser
Former Chairman and CEO

LOOKING FORWARD

When a company celebrates its centennial, the occasion serves to rekindle our interest in its history. For me, this interest is more than nostalgic; it's a key to understanding Weyerhaeuser—what we are today and the journey we have taken to get here—and a guide to help us navigate into the future. When I joined the company in 1997, I knew that Weyerhaeuser enjoyed a worldwide reputation for its values. In fact, those values drew me to the company and played a role in my decision to join it.

Traditions Through the Trees was one of the first projects suggested to me by George Weyerhaeuser, and my predecessor, Jack Creighton. This book explores company history through our values and the impact they have had on our customers, suppliers, shareholders, communities, and Weyerhaeuser people. The history of Weyerhaeuser is often told with the words of our colleagues. I believe it merits a close look.

Assisting in the development of this book has helped me understand the unique character of Weyerhaeuser. I have no doubt that, whether you are new to the company or have been associated with it for many years, you will discover just how unique our values are—and you'll probably find a few surprises, too.

I believe that *Traditions Through the Trees* will serve us and future generations as a reference to our past and a guide to our future. As we begin our second 100 years, it is important that we understand our values—the cornerstone of our "Roadmap for Success," which outlines our strategies for the next 10 years and beyond. With our values, our roadmap, and many dedicated colleagues, I know we will achieve our vision of being the best forest products company in the world and will prosper as we meet the challenges of the new century.

Sincerely,

Steven R. Rogel

Steven R. Rogel
Chairman, President, and CEO

Steven R. Rogel

7

The Value of Values

On an autumn afternoon in 1998, three men entered a wood-paneled Weyerhaeuser conference room, one after another. The eldest, tanned and animated, would speak for the past. The second, with the relaxed demeanor of recent retirement, represented the present. The third personified the future.

The senior member of the group was George H. Weyerhaeuser, a great-grandson of the company namesake, and the company's leader from 1966 to 1991. During 1990 and 1991, he and his successor, John W. "Jack" Creighton, led a thorough review of all the company's businesses and developed an updated set of strategies and plans for the future. The newcomer, Steven R. Rogel, had joined the company from Willamette Industries in 1997 to lead Weyerhaeuser into its second century.

As Weyerhaeuser's 100th anniversary approached in 2000, the three leaders met to send a message about the heritage of values that ties the company's past to its future.

"To put it simply," Rogel said, "the times have changed over a hundred years, but our values have endured."

"And that's in the face of the reality that an awful lot of things change," added George Weyerhaeuser, chairman of the board at the time, who spoke with the authority of his 50-year career.

"These values, because they have worked in the past, have stood the test of time," Creighton said. "This has been a big part of why the company has been successful and is still around, and [the values] will be, to a great degree, what guides the company into the future."

Opposite: Foresters identify trees for thinning, an important element in commercial forestry.

Shown (from left): President and Chief Executive Officer Steven R. Rogel, then-Chairman of the Board George H. Weyerhaeuser, and retired President and Chief Executive Officer John W. "Jack" Creighton in a September 1998 meeting where they discussed the origin of the company's values, their present use, and their likely effect on Weyerhaeuser's future.

What are Weyerhaeuser's values? Until 1991, each employee might have answered this question differently, although a few constant themes were apparent. "The company has always had a set of values, but those values were never put down on paper," Creighton explained.

That situation began changing in 1990 as Creighton, George Weyerhaeuser, and their management team planned strategic direction for the company. For the first time, the company's leaders resolved to capture its values in words that could be printed and posted in every corner of what had become a worldwide operation.

"It was worth some time to make sure we were all singing off the same song sheet," said Charles W. "Charley" Bingham, who was then executive vice president of Timberlands and

Wood Products. Many of Weyerhaeuser's decentralized businesses already had developed their own missions and beliefs. Creighton set out to build an umbrella of values that could encompass and strengthen that previous work.

Creighton enlisted a team to help with the project: Bingham; Norman E. Johnson, senior vice president of technology; John H. "Jack" Waechter, executive vice president of the Pulp, Paper and Packaging group; Steven R. Hill, senior vice president of human resources; and William C. Stivers, chief financial officer. William M. Shields, who joined the company from Willamette Industries to lead the wood products business, supplied a fresh perspective.

This team held brainstorming sessions and talked to employees throughout the company. What emerged in 1992 after a great deal of discussion and refinement was a list of values, set down in five categories:

CUSTOMERS.
We listen to our customers and improve our products and services to meet their present and future needs.

PEOPLE.
Our success depends on high-performing people working together in a safe and healthy workplace where diversity, development, and teamwork are valued and recognized.

ACCOUNTABILITY.

We expect superior performance and are accountable for our actions and results. Our leaders set clear goals and expectations, are supportive, and provide and seek frequent feedback.

CITIZENSHIP.

We support the communities where we do business, hold ourselves to the highest standards of ethical conduct and environmental responsibility, and communicate openly with Weyerhaeuser people and the public.

FINANCIAL RESPONSIBILITY.

We are prudent and effective in the use of the resources entrusted to us.

These values are linked. Viewed together, they express a legacy passed from one generation of Weyerhaeuser people to the next through the examples set by managers, loggers, foresters, salespeople, and mill hands.

"The value systems are basically family-based," Rogel said, "and they don't emanate from just one family." Cofounder Frederick Weyerhaeuser, his partners, and the company's first general manager, George S. Long, all imparted their high standards to the organization.

Rather than depending on iron-fisted authority, Frederick Weyerhaeuser used teamwork and folksy wisdom to bring others around to his viewpoint. He would tramp through a field of six-foot-high stumps from the previous winter's harvest and shake his head at the wood wasted there. The loggers knew it

was easier, particularly in deep snow, to cut high on the flared base of the tree. Frederick suggested that if they would cut the stumps a little lower, he could sit on them better.[1] Similar stories abound of Frederick's honesty, hard work, good humor, and aversion to waste.

George S. Long reinforced these qualities in the corporate culture. For instance, rather than involve brokers who might confuse property lines or inflate prices, he insisted on selling the company's logged lands directly to settlers, and then only when he could verify that they were well-informed and prepared for the hardships of farming. He took on this responsibility "not because we think it is the most economic thing to do, but because we think it is the right thing to do."[2]

Weyerhaeuser was recognized for its ethics in 1997, when the company received the American Business Ethics Award from the American Society of CLU and ChFC, a national association of certified life underwriters and chartered financial consultants.

11

Many of Weyerhaeuser's values came from family values that were first imprinted on the company by its founders, including (as shown from left) A. W. Laird, Frederick Weyerhaeuser, and P. M. Musser.

12

Management of the company's resources, including pruning of lower branches from plantation-grown pines in Weyerhaeuser forests, shown here in North Carolina, was an essential step in producing premium appearance-grade lumber for 21st-century markets.

"I believe integrity is the foundation," Creighton said, "and that the values are sometimes so natural you don't even think about them."

Sometimes—such as the occasion of a 100th birthday—you do. Dozens of Weyerhaeuser employees, from executives to receptionists, biologists, and machine operators, reflected on the company's values during interviews for this book. Many echoed the comment of Arkansas forester Kenny White, who said, "It sounds a little corny, but when we see that green logo—hell, I got a little bit of pride in that name."

Such pride is one benefit of the company's values. "I really underestimated the power of documenting the values," noted Stivers. "It has a profound effect in helping to bring the company together." Creighton said the values also provide a code of conduct against which individuals can check their own daily actions and those of the company.

Creighton agreed with George Weyerhaeuser and other leaders that the company's reputation for solid values also gives it an edge in the marketplace. As Stivers put it, "The Weyerhaeuser name opens a lot of doors."

Rogel took the idea further: "The values that a society has become your franchise to operate. Companies without values have difficulty over the long haul maintaining that franchise and staying in business." Rogel, charged with the company's future, hoped that this book would provide insight into its values and expectations so that everyone at Weyerhaeuser could understand how to contribute. He said, "It's doubly important to keep the things we've all defined as family values— transformed into company values—going."

"The purpose of looking back is to develop some sense of direction and continuity," said George Weyerhaeuser. "It is not only a matter of institutional memory. It's a strong statement of the kinds of people that we want to be."

People and values. That's where Weyerhaeuser's story began 100 years ago. That, too, was the foundation for the next 100.

A Brief History of Weyerhaeuser

In 100 years of operation, Weyerhaeuser Company produced more than its fair measure of legendary people and pioneering practices for the timber industry. It also grew mightily from its beginning with three employees in a turn-of-the-century office in Washington State. Weyerhaeuser Timber Company began in 1900 without mills and without products—just vast, mostly unmapped tracts of forestland and a vision of future growth. As the 20th century came to a close, nearly 45,000 people worked in a mosaic of Weyerhaeuser forests, offices, and manufacturing operations.

The company rose from humble beginnings. As a teenaged German immigrant in the 1850s, Frederick Weyerhaeuser began his life's work counting lumber for an Illinois sawmill.

In less than two years, his initiative gained him the chance to manage the lumberyard. Tough times forced the young manager to barter farm produce for lumber and to exchange the produce in turn for logs and supplies.[1] His success soon positioned him to buy the mill. He pooled funds with his brother-in-law, Frederick C. A. Denkmann, and formed Weyerhaeuser & Denkmann.

Honesty, hard work, and charm made Frederick a success. His workday sometimes began at two o'clock in the morning. Quoting from *Poor Richard's Almanack*, the lumberman known as "Dutch Fred" won friends and business associates. Together, Weyerhaeuser and Denkmann made wise investments in timber and sawmills along the Mississippi River and its tributaries.

Opposite: Loaded on a makeshift open-air railcar, loggers, shown here in 1904, were transported deep into Douglas fir and other mixed conifer forests, where they would labor for 10 hours. Eight-hour days became the standard for Weyerhaeuser employees in 1918.

15

In an industry of fiercely competitive individuals, Frederick favored cooperation as a path to innovation and greater success for everyone. For instance, each company traditionally branded its logs before floating them to its downstream mill. Each mill then sorted all the logs to recover its own. This system wasted labor and delayed all the logs at every mill. Instead, Frederick suggested scaling—judging the timber content—of each log as it went into the stream. Then each mill owner could recover equivalent timber rather than particular logs.

This 200-million-board-foot logjam was caused by an 1880s spring flood on the Saint Croix River in Wisconsin. It represented a test of the Frederick Weyerhaeuser plan for mill owners along the river to scale logs upstream before setting them afloat and then to retrieve a like amount when the logs reached their downriver mill sites.

The concept depended on honest scaling, with each participant trusting the others. Frederick readily persuaded his associates along the lower Mississippi to join in. Upstream mill owners balked—until nature gave them a push. Record flooding in 1880 swept a whole season's harvest downriver in a jumbled mess. Awash in competitors' logs, Frederick and his associates graciously traded timber they owned upstream to the northern mills in exchange for logs washed too far south. Impressed by this spirit of fairness, the upstream mill owners agreed to permanently adopt scaling. This reinforced Frederick's reputation for teamwork, innovation, and fair play.

By the turn of the 19th century, Frederick was looking for a new challenge. When neighbor and railroad magnate James J. Hill approached him about forestland in the Pacific Northwest, there was no shortage of interest—or investors. Weyerhaeuser Timber Company was incorporated on January 18, 1900, to purchase 900,000 acres of Washington forestland. For decades, the purchase would be the largest single private land transaction in U.S. history.[2] Even at the reasonable price of $6 per acre, one observer noted, it took "practically all the lumbermen on the upper Mississippi River to raise the money."[3]

Weyerhaeuser & Denkmann put up about one-third of the $5.4 million investment. Slightly less funding came from Laird, Norton & Company, a Minnesota lumber concern. Five of Frederick's associates—Laird, Norton

representative Robert Laird McCormick, Sumner T. McKnight, Orrin H. Ingram, and brothers Artemus and Lafayette Lamb— contributed from $300,000 to $350,000 each for about 5 percent of the company. Nine others bought smaller shares. The investors elected Frederick president and treasurer of the new company.

Frederick wanted to call it the Universal Timber Company, but his partners overruled him. Naming the company after Weyerhaeuser did more than honor their visionary friend and associate. The name carried a reputation for integrity and quality that immediately provided an advantage in the marketplace, in financial circles, and among the public. As Corporate Secretary W. L. McCormick later noted in discussing the name of a new subsidiary, "The name 'Weyerhaeuser' will have some advantage, in that it will insure a knowledge in the public mind that they are to be treated as Weyerhaeuser customers, or in other words fairly."[4] The founders didn't develop a statement of values for the new company. With the name Weyerhaeuser on the door, they apparently didn't feel they needed one.

For more than its first decade, Weyerhaeuser's primary business was timberland. Fate and fire pushed the company into harvesting and manufacturing sooner than some might have liked. A facility in Everett, Washington, was purchased in 1902, more for its deepwater harbor than for its sawmill. The same year, salvage logging began in southwestern Washington following the Yacolt Burn, a forest fire that damaged 23 square miles of company timberland. More than a decade would pass before another sawmill joined the system. A number of logging companies went to work in the 1910s and 1920s, however, organized through Weyerhaeuser Timber Company subsidiaries and joint ventures.

Difficult markets after World War I helped prompt research efforts to find uses for sawmill waste. Weyerhaeuser Timber Company first became involved in such research in 1917 through other companies owned by its founders. Weyerhaeuser Timber Company took a larger, more formal stake in that effort in 1921 by acquiring one-quarter of the Wood Conversion Company, newly formed to squeeze more value from every tree.

Left: Shown with two of their grandchildren in the yard of their St. Paul, Minnesota, home are Sarah and Frederick Weyerhaeuser in the early 1900s.

The Denkmanns, Anna Catherine and F. C. A. Anna Catherine was Sarah Weyerhaeuser's sister. Together, the families were partners in many business enterprises. F. C. A. was a founding shareholder and a member of Weyerhaeuser Timber Company's first board of directors.

17

The economic hard times starting in 1929 slowed but did not stop Weyerhaeuser's growth. New mills opened that year at Longview, Washington, and at Klamath Falls, Oregon. The Depression economy left a mark, however, as Weyerhaeuser focused even harder on increasing yield from its forests and mills. Timber Company pulping operations began in 1931 to use hemlock logs. Pres-to-logs®, invented in Idaho in 1929, turned more sawmill waste into a popular consumer product for fireplaces and campfires. Plywood and panels joined the product line with a 1940 acquisition. At the same time, Weyerhaeuser foresters worked to develop sustained-yield forestry. Their efforts reached a milestone in 1941 with the dedication in southwestern Washington of the company's Clemons Tree Farm, the nation's first certified tree farm.

Weyerhaeuser products for ships and warplanes had been a staple during World War I. For World War II, Weyerhaeuser contributed not only lumber but also ships and people. As a general agent of the War Shipping Administration, the Weyerhaeuser Steamship Company coordinated the military operation of dozens of steamships, including eight of its own. In the mills, women entered the work force as never before to maintain wartime production.

Following the war, the company had the resources to grow from a regional operation to a national presence. Weyerhaeuser bought 90,000 acres in Mississippi and Alabama in 1956. The expansion continued the following year with acquisition of a North Carolina

paper mill, more than three dozen container and carton plants across the country, and additional southern forestland from Kieckhefer Container and Eddy Paper Corporation. National advertising that featured forest wildlife helped make Weyerhaeuser a household name.

By 1959, that name was stamped on building materials, paper, shipping containers, and a host of other forest products. Dropping "Timber" from its identity, the company adopted its present logo. The green "tree in a triangle" would soon identify Weyerhaeuser around the world.

To find new markets for timber blown down in southwestern Washington during the 1962 Columbus Day storm, company sales teams turned to international customers. Offices opened in Japan, France, Belgium, Italy,

Opposite: In 1939, loggers walked among a Weyerhaeuser Timber Company stand of Douglas fir located in southwestern Washington.

Weyerhaeuser entered the container manufacturing business in 1957, producing corrugated shipping containers, paperboard, folding cartons, and milk cartons for such well-known customers as Quaker Oats.

19

and Australia. Exports increased, and so did customer demands. Weyerhaeuser soon began harvest operations in Indonesia, Malaysia, and the Philippines to supply Asian markets. Through joint ventures, the company began operating mills and converting plants in marketplaces ranging from nearby Canada to Europe, Africa, South America, and the Caribbean.

Back home, in 1963, the abbreviation WY took a place on the New York Stock Exchange and other U.S. exchanges. Though company stock had been available to the public, the exchange listing made transactions easier and stock values better known.

Frederick Weyerhaeuser's great-grandson George Weyerhaeuser became president in 1966. The fourth-generation leader announced a new approach to forest management: High Yield Forestry. This collection of intensive management techniques included soil preparation, seedling planting, brush control, fertilization, and thinning. Also utilizing genetic tree improvement and pruning, High Yield Forestry revolutionized commercial forestry by more than doubling the rate of wood growth on Weyerhaeuser forestland.

In the meantime, Weyerhaeuser both invested in its core businesses and increased its diversification. In 1967, the company began operating a sawmill in Philadelphia, Mississippi, its first in that state. Weyerhaeuser entered the home-building business in 1969 with the acquisitions of Quadrant Corporation of Washington and Pardee Construction Company and its sister mortgage company in California. Annual Weyerhaeuser sales hit $1 billion that year. That autumn, Weyerhaeuser

Weyerhaeuser began acquiring southern pine forests in 1956, when it purchased forestlands in Mississippi and Alabama. Shown is a pine plantation near New Bern, North Carolina.

made its single-largest land purchase ever when it acquired 1.8 million acres of Arkansas and Oklahoma forestland and several sawmills and paper mills from Dierks Forests. Other investments during the next decade led first to products such as diapers and newsprint and later to businesses as diverse as ski resorts, garden supply, financial services, and salmon ranching.

During the 1970s profits climbed, international markets blossomed, and the company built an award-winning new headquarters building in Federal Way, Washington. And society was changing. Before the first Earth Day in 1970, Weyerhaeuser already had spent more than $100 million on innovative pollution controls. The amount increased rapidly over the following decades in order to meet tightening regulatory requirements.

By the mid-1970s, the company had withdrawn from most of its harvesting operations in Southeast Asia because of increased concern about environmental impacts, political strife, and the challenge of conducting business in the

region according to the company's ethical standards. On home soil, Weyerhaeuser fought or settled a number of antitrust suits, a reflection of its growing size. Nonetheless, the company continued to grow, with new customers in China, its first paper-recycling operations, more than $3 billion in capital investments, and the opening of a research center in Federal Way. As the 1970s wound down, Weyerhaeuser sales hit the $4 billion mark and employment reached a high of more than 47,800.

Although the company had made great strides in protecting its forestland from fires and insects, catastrophic natural events still occurred. No amount of planning could have prepared Weyerhaeuser for the eruption of Mount St. Helens on May 18, 1980. The volcanic explosion devastated 68,000 acres of company forestland. While the mountain

Left: Shown (from left) are Dierks Forests employees B. F. Williams, J. J. Jordan, Mill Superintendent F. H. Singletary, R. H. Windle, and Mill General Superintendent J. C. Plumlee before a 1957 tour of the Dierks kraft paper mill located at Pine Bluff, Arkansas.

Logs and trucks were strewn downriver by a flash flood on the Toutle River following the May 1980 eruption of Mount St. Helens.

Weyerhaeuser began to establish a relationship with the People's Republic of China when the resumption of trade between the two countries was approved in June 1971. Shown is a Chinese delegation at the opening of the company's Beijing office in 1984. In 1998, the company opened a corrugated container manufacturing plant in Shanghai as part of a joint venture with SCA of Sweden. A second SCA Weyerhaeuser packaging plant opened in Wuhan in 1999.

Premium sake packaging was produced in Japan by Weyerhaeuser in partnership with Nippon Paper Industries. This relationship began in 1973, when Weyerhaeuser and Jujo Paper Company (later renamed Nippon) entered into a partnership that in 1976 became known as NORPAC.

Opposite: Rolls of lightweight coated paper were temporarily stored awaiting shipment to printers from Weyerhaeuser's Columbus, Mississippi, fine paper mill.

continued to rumble, inflation and rising mortgage rates caused markets for building materials to sink to their lowest levels since the Great Depression. An economy in recession and unfavorable exchange rates sent the company's pulp and paper markets into a slump.

As company employees worked to salvage timber mowed down by the volcano's blast, Weyerhaeuser leaders worked to trim the business and improve results. The least successful operations, including several Northwest wood products mills, were sold or closed. Western wood products and timberlands employees were cut back as operations were curtailed, and the company's salaried work force shrank by 25 percent.

The tough competition of the 1980s brought renewed attention to quality and customer service. By the end of the decade, the company determined that it had diversified into businesses in which it could not grow sufficiently or successfully. Weyerhaeuser

returned to its roots. Chairman of the Board George Weyerhaeuser initiated the refocusing effort, and was joined by Jack Creighton, who had been named president and chief operating officer in 1988. While the company continued to invest in its core businesses—newsprint, corrugated packaging, building materials, paper, forestland—it sold other operations. Businesses involved in gypsum wallboard, fish farming, garden supplies, milk cartons, annuities, and home construction were among those sold, further reducing the work force by 8,300 people.

Weyerhaeuser emerged in the early 1990s with a vision of its goal for the future: becoming the best forest products company in the world. Strategies were developed to focus the company's operations on a narrowed base. Throughout the decade, Weyerhaeuser worked to improve its financial success and to reaffirm its leadership in forest research, manufacturing, environmental performance, and product quality. Committed to serving customers wherever they might go, the company again began to invest in Asian operations as well as forestland in the Southern Hemisphere.

Steve Rogel joined the company in December 1997 from Willamette Industries, one of the forest products industry's leading companies. As Weyerhaeuser's president and chief executive officer, Rogel cautiously began focusing the company's operations and culture in preparation for the challenges of the 21st century and its second hundred years. In April 1999 he assumed the added responsibility of serving as chairman of Weyerhaeuser's board.

CHAPTER ONE

A Sense of Family

Flags flew at half-staff at Weyerhaeuser locations around the United States in 1997. In a small town in North Carolina, a traffic accident had taken the lives of 10 teenagers. Almost all of the victims were the children or other relatives of employees at Weyerhaeuser's Plymouth complex. Jack Creighton, company president, rearranged his schedule and flew across the country to express support to the grieving families.

This response to tragedy reveals one of Weyerhaeuser's most deeply rooted values. Weyerhaeuser managers call it respect for people. Many employees refer to it as being a family. By the end of the 20th century, counting retirees, spouses, and children, more than 200,000 people considered themselves part of the Weyerhaeuser Company family. Many employees said that's what they liked best about Weyerhaeuser. "It's the family atmosphere," said Regina Ciupitu, a 20-year employee in Hot Springs, Arkansas. "Everybody rallies together."

Business at Weyerhaeuser is built on personal relationships. The company is well known for a chain of leaders directly descended from founders, but it's not only the corporate leadership that passes from parent to child. Three and four generations of Weyerhaeuser employees have sawed lumber and made paper from North Carolina to British Columbia. Customers become part of the family, with ties that endure for decades.

In 1987, George Weyerhaeuser cited the attitude of Weyerhaeuser people as the one thing he most hoped had been maintained during his tenure. "Before I became president,

Selling lumber, like milling it, was a skill passed along from generation to generation. Shown in 1933 instructing his children on the fine points of quality lumber is third-generation lumber merchant Herbert Porter in the yard of the Porter Lumber Company, a Morenci, Michigan, 4-Square dealer.

25

Shown sitting in front of a Frederick Weyerhaeuser portrait in a 1930s C. H. Wiesmer photograph are (from left) F. E. Weyerhaeuser, J. P. Weyerhaeuser, C. A. Weyerhaeuser, and R. M. Weyerhaeuser. J. P. Weyerhaeuser was the company's president from 1914 to 1928, and F. E. Weyerhaeuser was Weyerhaeuser Timber Company president from 1934 to 1945.

George S. Long, shown in his Tacoma, Washington, office, was Weyerhaeuser Timber Company's first general manager. He was succeeded in 1929 by F. Rodman Titcomb. Long died in 1930.

there was an overwhelming feeling of the people who worked for this company that it was absolutely the greatest place to work," he said. "That said something about their personal commitment and the way they had been treated. If I had a wish, it would be that I can sustain that feeling about the company by the people who *are* the company."[1]

Employee attitudes about Weyerhaeuser have been shaped partly by wages and benefits that have generally led the industry. Weyerhaeuser is one of only 55 companies, and the only forest products firm, to be included in both the 1984 and 1993 editions of *The 100 Best Companies to Work for in America*. Weyerhaeuser was rated especially highly for benefits, employee pride, and a "tradition of caring."

FAMILY PHILOSOPHY

Weyerhaeuser's family philosophy descends from founder Frederick Weyerhaeuser. Frederick believed in teamwork. Claiming that he'd rather own a one-sixth share in each of six businesses than a company of his own,[2] he proved the point by becoming involved in more than 50 companies and subsidiaries.[3] Frederick set the tone for such ventures, including the Mississippi River Logging Company, which he created in 1870. One of its 17 owners, Matthew Norton, would later recall that "members of this company were more like brothers in their intercourse with one another than would be found in most organizations for profit."[4]

On Frederick's authorization, in early 1900, Weyerhaeuser Timber Company hired its first employee, George S. Long, to manage its Pacific Northwest affairs. Long was known for his intelligence, integrity, loyalty, and gift for managing people.[5] In this way, he was an echo of Frederick in shaping the new company's culture. Long was referring to the sawmill in Snoqualmie Falls, Washington, but he could have been talking about the whole company when he reminded a new manager in 1925 that the goal was to create "a good working family organization that would work harmoniously together in an effective way."[6]

Back in 1900, Long wasted little time setting up shop in Rooms 19 and 20 of the Northern Pacific Building in Tacoma, Washington. He hired a mapmaker and a bookkeeper, and by the end of the year a dozen people were working for Weyerhaeuser Timber Company. Most were cruisers, who traveled the forests, assessing the value of the company's timber. Long looked for cruisers who were honest, intelligent, discreet, observant, and loyal—and in tip-top physical trim to maneuver in the forest's heavy undergrowth. Long's philosophy was to "give a certain territory to a man, and have him look after it, so that he could make his home at some central point, and depend upon not being very far away from his family."[7]

Two events in 1902 rapidly increased the number of people working on behalf of Weyerhaeuser Timber Company. The first was the acquisition of a sawmill in Everett, Washington. Along with the mill came a logging company, a dormant shipyard, and dozens of employees and contract loggers. The second event was the Yacolt fire in September of the same year, which charred 23 square miles of company forestland in southwestern Washington.[8]

Salvage logging began immediately after the fire, before powder-post beetles, pine borers, and other insects could speed the wood's decay. Logging camps sprang up from Puget Sound to the Columbia River, with scores of people felling and sawing Weyerhaeuser timber. Though the work was backbreaking, there was no shortage of people ready to pick up a saw. Before 1920, skilled tree fallers might earn

from $3.00 to $4.50 a day—more than double the wages for farm labor.[9,10] Even a young message runner could earn a dollar a day plus board and a camp bed.[11]

In the early years, the beds were simply straw-covered bunks, but workers got all they could eat: three meals a day of beef and bacon, fresh fruit, vegetables, pastries, and plenty of coffee. Some called such menus "extravagant" fare.[12] Food aside, the camps could be rough. Logger Russ Carmichael got his first taste of a logging camp during a 1909 visit at the tender age of seven. Young Russ found himself flung onto an upper bunk for safety and "a ringside seat" when a knife fight broke out in the bunkhouse. Like other loggers who worked as contracted labor, he would later sample many

Weyerhaeuser Timber Company's first mill, acquired from the Bell-Nelson Company in 1902, was located in Everett, Washington. It was an old mill purchased mostly for its deep tidewater site.

27

Weyerhaeuser Timber Company

18244

companies and camps, including more than
20 in one month. He claimed that the
Weyerhaeuser camps were "better than the
great majority."[13]

During Weyerhaeuser's early decades,
employee ranks also grew at new sawmills, first
in Washington and then in Oregon. If there
wasn't already a community nearby,
Weyerhaeuser—like other companies of the
time—built one. At Snoqualmie Falls, for
instance, Long aimed to "build it up in a way
that would have an appeal to those employed
by the company." He pressed for family homes
with individuality, not cookie-cutter barracks.[14]

Snoqualmie Falls was an
isolated community, and the
company offered many ameni-
ties to attract and benefit its
employees, including a variety
of housing, athletic facilities,
a hospital, schools, a company
store, and a community center
where dances were held for
employees and their families.

Along with the homes came a boardinghouse, a
hospital, a community center, and a company
store. The community center offered dances,
"moving pictures," and other entertainment.
Managers hoped such offerings would be
"powerful factors in overcoming the restless,
roving, reckless spirit now possessing many
of our men."[15]

Early in the 1900s, ideas of socialism and com-
munism began filtering through the United
States. Labor organizations formed to work for
better wages and conditions. About 1912,
the Wobblies (more formally known as the
Industrial Workers of the World [IWW]) began
shouting from soapboxes on Everett street
corners. Their goals were to overthrow
capitalism, abolish the wage system, and force
the "complete surrender of all control of
industry to the organized workers."[16]

The discontent struck a chord among
employees everywhere, including at
Weyerhaeuser, in spite of the fact that logging
camp amenities had improved and wages had
risen. In 1917, in fact, company operations in
the Northwest had some of the highest sawmill
wages in the country. But the cost of living and
people's expectations had risen, too. The rela-
tive shortage of workers caused by World War I
gave people in the U.S. labor force more power
than they'd ever enjoyed. In 1917, with support
from the Wobblies as well as young chapters of
the American Federation of Labor (AFL) and
the International Union of Timber Workers,
major strikes shut down most Northwest
operations, including Weyerhaeuser's. Typical
demands for industry employees included
showers in logging camps, minimum wages of
$3.00 or $3.50 a day, Sundays off, eight- or
nine-hour days, and free hospital care.[17] Since
Weyerhaeuser already provided above-average
wages and working conditions, the main issue
was shorter workdays. But the industry was

already struggling to provide the lumber needed for warships and planes. The government stepped in, and uniformed soldiers worked alongside loggers. The War Department helped organize employees and companies into the 4-L, the Loyal Legion of Loggers and Lumbermen, as an alternative to the unions. By the end of the decade, the Wobblies were on the way out, and other unions, including the AFL and the Congress of Industrial Organizations (CIO), were taking their place. Most of the employees' earlier demands had been implemented by employers, however, and eight-hour days were common. Toward the end of the Depression, government observers noted that the Weyerhaeuser Timber Company paid the highest wages in the industry anywhere in the world.[18]

FAMILY LOYALTY

The 1917 strike wouldn't be the last for Weyerhaeuser Timber Company. The Great Depression that lingered through the 1930s and the inflationary markets of the 1950s, 1970s, and early 1980s, in particular, prompted several

lengthy strikes. For managers who felt close to employees, it sometimes was hard not to take these disputes personally. As he watched picketers assemble for a 1935 strike, Harry Morgan Sr., the Longview facility manager, recalled how he had helped some employees get credit for groceries, found jobs for many during the Depression, and played baseball with others. "I can't understand it," he said. "Why have these men turned against me?"[19]

In fact, whether they were involved in labor disputes or not, most Weyerhaeuser employees continued to be loyal. Joe Lebo, one of the first log unloaders at the new Longview facility, said proudly, "That's where I put in almost 28 years."[20] He and his contemporaries were satisfied and proud to remain in their jobs for decades, and many worked 45 or 50 years before retiring. As 25-year employee Herb Muise quipped, "I even bleed green."

For their part, company leaders in times of economic trouble successfully argued for maintaining wages, delaying market-related

West Coast lumber, including Douglas fir and spruce, was considered critical during World War I, and when coastal supplies of lumber for everything from ship decks to airplane manufacturing were threatened by strikes, the government stepped in and uniformed soldiers worked alongside loggers. Shown (from left) are district logging superintendent John Yeon, Lieutenant Colonel Hill, and Captain Hayden during a tour of coastal logging operations.

31

Shown is a 1935 Longview mill walkout at the beginning of a strike that was later resolved with an improved wage and benefit package for the mill's employees.

The Depression severely affected the forest products industry during the early 1930s. Unemployed loggers sometimes found work with federal agency programs, such as the Works Progress Administration, doing forest conservation work.

Daring high-climbers scaled giant trees with saw and ax, topped them to make spar trees, then assisted in rigging cables used for yarding logs from surrounding stands of trees. In the company's early decades, the tallest trees reached heights of 250 feet or more.

shutdowns, and improving working conditions.[21] As the United States sank into the Great Depression in 1929, nearly 40,000 Northwest loggers and mill hands lost their jobs.[22] The number of people employed by Weyerhaeuser dropped only from 7,500 in 1929 to 6,735 in 1938, although at times their working hours were reduced to almost nothing.

Ted Durment, employment manager at the Klamath Falls, Oregon, mill during the Depression, recalled saving lumber orders to make a full day's work. "Then I'd have to go out and round up the men," he said. Because employees could no longer afford telephone service, Durment traveled from house to house. "Maybe a fellow would be sitting dejectedly on the porch. I'd say, 'Come to work on Wednesday,' and his face would light up. You'd think I'd given him a million dollars."[23]

As prosperity slowly returned, Weyerhaeuser added major employee benefits such as retirement pensions, paid vacations, and holidays. The company initiated other benefits, such as scholarships for employees' children. As early as 1929, profit-sharing plans were introduced for some salaried employees. Newly formed credit unions formalized an unwritten employee benefit, according to Woods Manager Alden Jones. He said that the Longview credit union "really got started because the company was making a great number of loans to the workers, and [local manager] Harry Morgan Sr. felt that the company shouldn't be in the finance business."[24]

By 1948 more than 12,000 people were taking home a Weyerhaeuser paycheck. Second- and third-generation employees turned out products under the guidance of a third-generation leader, Phil Weyerhaeuser, a grandson of Frederick. And Weyerhaeuser, employees recalled, took care of its own. Scott Marshall remembered when his father, who was employed by the Wood Conversion Company, died in 1963. Only 17, Marshall became head of his family. With help from his uncle, a long-time Weyerhaeuser sales representative, the company created a job for him. "They put side-boards around us," Marshall said. After stints at school and in the military, "I literally sent one résumé." Now vice president of policy, finance and strategic planning for Weyerhaeuser Timberlands and Wood Products, he said, "Weyerhaeuser was where I was destined."

By and large, Weyerhaeuser leaders were ahead of the times in guarding the health of employees. At Everett, employees were able to take advantage of a group hospital plan (one of the first in the industry) in 1908.[25] Over the next 25 years, employee benefits expanded and Weyerhaeuser Timber Company became the first forest products firm in the Northwest to adopt group health, accident, and life insurance plans.[26] In the mid-1930s, the company began giving employees physical exams. Alden Jones recalled two young doctors who hiked into the woods to examine him and his crew. The doctors, unable to keep up with their trail-hardened patients, pronounced them all healthy and limped home.[27]

The company's early focus on health benefits coincided with the hazards of the work. Weyerhaeuser supervisors encouraged their teams to consider safety, and some held weekly safety meetings. The words of logging foreman Jack Arnold, who was known for his crew's safety performance, underline just how far safety processes have come since the 1930s. According to Russ Carmichael, Arnold once summed up his crew's secret at a camp meeting by saying, "I just holler to the sons of bitches, 'Run or die, you bastards,' and there ain't nobody in my crew ever goes to sleep and gets hurt."[28]

Safety improved dramatically over the years with better logging equipment and techniques. Formal Weyerhaeuser safety programs began in the 1940s. The biggest shift, however, was in attitudes. Longview sawmill employee Roscoe Howard said, "The turning point was when they finally learned that the only way to stop the accidents was to get each man involved. When he became part of the program (not the object of it) then your program began to get results."[29]

Safety also became a family concern. In 1964, Weyerhaeuser's Millicoma Tree Farm managers in Oregon invited employees' spouses for a firsthand view of the job, then asked them to give employees safety reminders on the way to work or in lunches brought from home.[30] Safety awareness efforts like this paid off. By the late 1960s, Weyerhaeuser had the best safety performance in the industry and repeatedly earned awards from the National Safety Council.[31] In 1971, on the basis of hours worked, Weyerhaeuser loggers had fewer accidents than its sales force.[32]

Throughout the 1980s the company continued to significantly improve its safety numbers, driven by the growing conviction that accidents were never inevitable. With this new mind-set, work teams stopped expecting or tolerating even a single accident, and in 1993 President Jack Creighton announced that safety was the company's top priority. Managers and employees performed safety audits and changed processes to further improve safety results. That year more than 100 locations worked without a lost-time accident. During the 1990s, a dozen Weyerhaeuser operations worked a million employee-hours or more

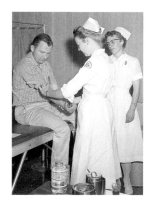

Shown is a company-run health-care facility during the 1930s. Weyerhaeuser recognized the need for medical care and offered a group hospital plan, one of the first in the industry, in 1908.

33

Following pages: In 1993 Weyerhaeuser's giant Columbus, Mississippi, pulp and paper complex received the prestigious Star designation, the highest award given by the U.S. Occupational Safety and Health Administration's Voluntary Protection Program for workplace safety.

Frederick Weyerhaeuser first invested in southern pine timberland with his Rock Island partners in 1882. Weyerhaeuser Company did not invest in the fast-growing timberlands of the South until its purchase of Alabama and Mississippi timberlands in 1956. Its largest purchase was that of Dierks Forests in 1969, which included mills and 1.8 million acres in Oklahoma and Arkansas. Weyerhaeuser's plans for the Dierks operations included the addition of a containerboard mill, shown here under construction in 1971. When it started up later that year, the mill featured a containerboard machine that at the time was the largest in the world.

without a lost-time accident. The U.S. Occupational Safety and Health Administration granted its prestigious Star designation, the agency's highest award for workplace safety, to the company's pulp and paper mill in Columbus, Mississippi; containerboard mill in Valliant, Oklahoma; customer service center in Cleveland, Ohio; Flint River pulp mill in Oglethorpe, Georgia; and lumber facility in Barnesville, Georgia.

WELCOME . . . AND SOMETIMES GOOD-BYE

Thousands of employees joined the Weyerhaeuser fold through acquisitions made in the 1950s and later. Among the largest were the purchases of Kieckhefer Container and Eddy Paper Corporation in 1957, Dierks Forests in 1969, several Procter & Gamble facilities and timber holdings in 1992, and MacMillan Bloedel in 1999. In most cases, Weyerhaeuser's reputation preceded it.

"We felt it was as good a company as you could find about taking care of their employees," said Land/Timber Manager Jerry Ragland. Ragland worked for Dierks Forests until 1969, when Weyerhaeuser purchased the company's Oklahoma and Arkansas forestland and several mills. The facilities employed more than 3,000 people. Weyerhaeuser was known to treat people well, but its new southern employees were unsure of the "big, anonymous company" and how it would fit into local culture. Over the following three decades, however, those employees and many more saw Weyerhaeuser fulfill its promises and put down long-term roots.

Compatible cultures are among the considerations in any Weyerhaeuser acquisition. Bill Corbin, executive vice president of Wood Products, said the people and skills joining Weyerhaeuser during an acquisition are crucial to successful long-term operations. "A collaborative approach takes the best from both [companies]," he said. The company used this approach in acquiring facilities and companies through the years, including Procter & Gamble mills in 1992 and the acquisition of Cavenham timberland and sawmills in Mississippi and Louisiana in 1996.

Weyerhaeuser's concern for people is sometimes viewed unfavorably by the investment community, which has criticized the company for not being faster to sell or shut down poorly performing facilities.[33] When difficult business decisions cost jobs, Weyerhaeuser employees receive severance pay and help in finding other work. Nevertheless, divestments are difficult. "You fire team members and friends, and it's tough," said Don Dale, timberlands manager in Mountain Pine, Arkansas.

More than 10,000 people left Weyerhaeuser's employ between 1988 and 1993 as the company divested itself of several of the product lines it didn't consider to be core forest products businesses. When operations were to close, the company made the announcements months in advance, set up outplacement centers, created an internal job-matching service, and granted severance packages that would give employees, in George Weyerhaeuser's words, "some opportunity to make a bridge to a new employer." In many cases, employees stayed with their new employers without changing jobs. "Most of the businesses have been sold to well-qualified buyers," George Weyerhaeuser said. "We're not going to sell our businesses to companies that have no prospect of carrying them on."

The divestments and layoffs did affect Weyerhaeuser's image as a dependable place to work. In the mid-1990s, a North Carolina junior-college professor told Bobby Freeman, human resources manager in Mountain Pine, Arkansas, that he'd stopped recommending Weyerhaeuser to students because everyone recruited from his institution worked for the company less than five years. But Freeman said the company had recaptured its momentum and he again received many inquiries from

students and would-be employees. Michael Garrett, quality/technical services manager of the pulp mill in New Bern, North Carolina, said, "Ten years ago, we took who we could get. The ones who interview with us now are the brightest and the best."

EMPLOYEES AS PARTNERS

Historically, traditional attitudes often prevailed that production employees, while essential, were not partners who could understand economic realities and help improve the business. "We went through a period where we said the employee was the problem," noted George Henson, retired vice president of manufacturing and Total Quality for Weyerhaeuser's pulp and paper business. This misconception extended to unions. Tom Luthy, retired senior vice president for Wood Products, said, "Until fairly recently, unions could never be viewed as allies."

The company introduced a new set of labor relations principles in 1994, which include the following:

1. We share the vision of a profitable and competitive business enterprise that serves the interests and needs of all stakeholders.

2. We will interact with each other and build relationships based on trust, honesty, openness, and mutual respect.

3. We will cooperate and emphasize problem-solving in addressing areas of mutual interest and concern.

Clay Burnett was a proud Dallas, Texas-based representative of Dierks Forests in 1966.

4. We accept the principle of continuous improvement through employee empowerment and empowerment as the means by which we will achieve our shared vision.

5. Management acknowledges and respects the role of the union in representing the interests of employees who have chosen it as their bargaining representative.

The principles were developed with input from employees and union leaders, then signed by Creighton and the national heads of the United Paperworkers International Union, the International Association of Machinists, and the Graphic Communications International Union. The three unions represented more than 80 percent of Weyerhaeuser's unionized employees. According to the company's 1994 annual report, "In union-represented facilities, labor relations principles state a joint union/management commitment to employee empowerment and involvement."

"We did that one right," said Marvin Waters, a leader in the development of the principles as vice president of corporate labor relations at that time. "Public principles keep you honest, and I think the principles will be viewed through time as one of the better things we've done to demonstrate the company's commitment to treating people with respect."

In the late 1990s, union members and company managers from coast to coast agreed that their relationships had greatly improved. Jerry Adams, a paper machine backtender at the North Bend, Oregon, containerboard mill, noted a decline in the "us versus them" mentality between management and employees. "You can't have that today," he said. "We're all here for the same reason— to make money for us and for the investors— and we'd better work together."[34]

Information sharing continued to grow, and in 1995 virtually every employee received a personal stake in the company's financial success through a profit-sharing plan. The plan pays in Weyerhaeuser stock, which is held for employees until they retire or leave the company. "We believe that by making employees owners of the company, we improve Weyerhaeuser's ability to realize its vision," Creighton said in the annual report. Nancy Crisp, president of OPEIU (Office and Professional Employees Industrial Union) Local 354 in Plymouth, North Carolina, called the Performance Share Plan "an effort to make each of us feel like part of the Weyerhaeuser family."[35]

Shown above is one of Frederick Weyerhaeuser's original stock certificates.

39

Opposite: Shown is Jerry Priebe, inspecting First Choice paper prior to its sheeting and packaging at the Rothschild, Wisconsin, mill.

TEAM BUILDING

John W. "Jack" Creighton served as Weyerhaeuser's president from 1989 until his retirement on December 1, 1997.

40

NORPAC began producing newsprint in 1979. Shown is President George Weyerhaeuser in 1980 on a tour of the Yomiuri Shimbun *pressroom, where he watched as Japanese newspapers were printed at a rate of 120,000 copies an hour.*

Reflecting business approaches of the times, generations of Weyerhaeuser managers have been comfortable as the commanders of traditional hierarchies. Michael Garrett, who joined the New Bern mill in 1980, said, "I came up at a time when you didn't question anything. It was 'yes sir, no sir.' "

"We were asking employees to check their brains at the gate," said George Henson. Henson, who became vice president of the New Bern mill in 1982, was one of the company's pioneers in developing a different attitude toward employees. The difference became apparent to Mardy Irby, a process control engineer at New Bern, who recalled a manager at her former company throwing his hard hat the length of the room when something went wrong. It took her a while to get used to Weyerhaeuser. "I'd been here about a month when we had a welding incident. Everyone was running around, working together to fix it. The phone started ringing, and I didn't want to answer it because I knew

it would be the mill manager. I figured he'd be yelling." She finally wondered aloud, "Why isn't George down here cussing at everyone?" A coworker told her that their mill manager knew they were handling it.

Trust is the core of employee empowerment. "It feels good to know the company trusts you enough to let you do your job," said Jimmy "Red" Wyatt, a storeroom clerk at Valliant. Working without a supervisor, Wyatt and his teammates made changes that saved the Oklahoma mill approximately half a million dollars.[36] Similarly, in Kamloops, British Columbia, an employee problem-solving team improved management of the mill's supply inventories in 1995 and cut inbound freight costs $15,000 in its first four months.[37]

Some employees who were told what to do for 20 years or more weren't always comfortable with changes in supervision, seniority systems, or responsibilities. Managers also felt the discomfort of change, a process that takes time and effort from everyone. During the mid-1990s, Lynchburg, Virginia, corrugated packaging plant leaders realized they had a few rules that had outlived their usefulness. For instance, employees had to show written proof of a death before they were permitted to take time for a family funeral. Robert Lovelady, then Lynchburg's production manager, said, "Inadvertently, we weren't treating people with the respect and dignity they deserved."[38]

The transition to high-performance work systems is easier in locations where the team philosophy can be built in from the ground up. The company began creating nontraditional work teams in the late 1970s, starting at NORPAC (North Pacific Paper Corp.), a joint venture in Longview, Washington. When the Columbus, Mississippi, pulp and paper mill and the Grayling, Michigan, oriented strand board (OSB) mill opened in 1982, employees signed on with the understanding that they would be problem-solvers, risk-takers, and team players. From the beginning, these mills have been among the company's manufacturing leaders.

Newer locations are accelerating Weyerhaeuser's shift to high-performance work teams. The company's OSB mill in Sutton, West Virginia, which started up in 1996, uses cross-training and job titles such as operations team member. "The teams here make our jobs easy because the mix of ideas always comes up with ways to work better or solve problems," said Soupy Campbell, an operations team member at Sutton. "The proof is that the mill is already performing better than anyone expected."[39]

WELCOMING DIVERSITY

Start-up operations also led Weyerhaeuser in another area of emphasis: increasing employee diversity. More than half of the managers at the company's sawmill in Greenville, North Carolina, are women or minorities. Weyerhaeuser's progressive attitude was made clear as early as 1924. Ku Klux Klan supporters

had just won local elections in Klamath Falls, Oregon, where Weyerhaeuser Timber Company hoped to build a mill. George S. Long called the news "disappointing and disgusting."[40]

When Weyerhaeuser shifted from regional to national operations, the company acquired facilities in communities with more diverse ethnic backgrounds. Human Resources Manager Bobby Freeman joined the company through such an acquisition in 1968. At that time, the company had very few minority employees, particularly in supervisory or management roles. "It was not a pretty picture," said Freeman, an African-American with experience in human relations roles at several Weyerhaeuser facilities.

As the civil rights movement hit full stride, Weyerhaeuser facilities formed human relations committees and began mentoring programs for minority college students. In 1970, at a box

In 1996, operations team member Soupy Campbell sat at the controls of the high-tech log-sorting equipment at the resource end of the company's oriented strand board (OSB) plant in Sutton, West Virginia.

41

War bonds raised billions, one dollar at a time, and Weyerhaeuser employees exceeded company, community, and national expectations for their support during World War II. Some crews donated part or all of a given day's pay to the war effort; formed "bicycle brigades" to conserve auto fuel and rubber; or suggested innovative ways to conserve vital materials around the workplace. And everyone worked hard to provide needed lumber. The Longview, Washington, lumber division in 1943 was the nation's first lumber plant to earn the U.S. Army/Navy "E" Award for excellent production performance during the war.

42

Motivated by patriotism and encouraged by wages in excess of a dollar an hour, women entered the work force in numbers that were unheard of before the outbreak of World War II. Shown are women working on the Snoqualmie Falls lumber mill green chain, a job that demanded strength and endurance.

plant in Closter, New Jersey, that employed a growing number of workers who spoke only Spanish, employees voted whether to have the supervisors learn Spanish or to learn English themselves. As a result, the plant began holding English classes three days a week. Word got around, and job applicants came to the plant specifically because of the class.[41]

Like other companies, Weyerhaeuser has had to overcome the challenges of establishing a diverse work force. "We went through the heartache of trying to get people in their rightful place," recalled Marvin Waters. Early in his career, Waters helped merge the separate bargaining units representing African-American and Caucasian employees at the Plymouth complex in North Carolina.

Before long, Waters and others also pursued the ideal of equality for women employees. Because the forest products industry began as a dangerous, muscle-pumping, sweat-driven frontier endeavor, it has been called second only to steel mills for its machismo. Early in the century, women had no part in logging, but served as secretaries, switchboard operators, and camp waitresses also known as "flunkies."

World War II created a shortage of workers along with a national need to produce lumber for military efforts. Women known popularly as "Pauline Bunyans" or "lumberettes" filled sawmill jobs vacated when men were sent to war. Some of the new workers earned compliments along the lines of, "The best man we ever had on that job was a woman."[42]

The changing nature of the work force was one of many things that helped prompt automation. Hank Stratton, an Everett pulp mill employee responsible for hauling the limestone rock used in making pulping chemicals, recalled, "Before I went into the service . . . we used to pick these big rocks up. That sure was hard on a man's back. After I came home they had a nice hoist rigged up for them."[43] Such innovations improved efficiency.

After the war, some women lost their jobs to the returning men, but many continued to work, and others joined them. By 1949, almost half of the employees of the Klamath Falls box "shook," or parts, factory were women, and the company's female staff included an engineer and a research Ph.D.[44] The trend continued over the following decades. "I was going to work for Weyerhaeuser just one year—long enough to buy some lawn furniture," laughed Martha Dowdy, a 30-year employee at Dierks. "I stayed because I liked it—and I still haven't bought that lawn furniture!"

By 1960, the company employed about 2,000 women in a work force of more than 20,000. Virtually every Weyerhaeuser operation had female employees in important production, research, and office positions. Gender distinctions were usually subtle, as in a 1969 employee survey that asked if Weyerhaeuser was "a place where I would like my son to work"—making no mention of daughters.

Today, like many other businesses, Weyerhaeuser still has a preponderance of white male employees, but the climate of the workplace has changed. "I've spent most of my career on work teams where I was the only woman. That's changing," said Rhonda Hunter, who joined the company in 1987 as an accountant and who now works in forestry. "Weyerhaeuser was willing to give me opportunities and allow me to grow in a nontraditional career path."

Curt Brown, a process engineer who began work at the New Bern mill during the 1990s, said he was drawn to the company partly because of its attitude toward diversity. "Weyerhaeuser was one of the first companies that offered me an internship," explained Brown, who is African-American. The magazine *U.S. Black Engineer* recognized the company's progress in 1998 when it named Weyerhaeuser one of America's top employers of African-American technical talent.

"If we're going to be the best, we have to hire the best," said Steve Hill, senior vice president of human resources. "We have to find a way to respect the diversity of each person and gain advantages from common and reliable processes."

Weyerhaeuser Technology Center lab technician Pamela Gibson loads an auto sampler for TKN (Total Kjeldahl Nitrogen) and phosphorus analysis. This assessment is used to determine the organic nitrogen content of pine needles, and the information gleaned assists foresters in regulating the frequency and amount of fertilizer needed to maximize tree growth.

INTERNAL COMPETITION

From the beginning, Weyerhaeuser has been a collection of different organizations and cultures. Because the company's founders believed strongly in partnerships and decentralization, early logging operations and sawmills were separate companies.

"We treat each company somewhat as a free lance and let each secure its best source for buying and selling," explained George S. Long in 1914.[45] As a result, Weyerhaeuser subsidiary mills sometimes competed with one another.

The Longview pulp mill started up as the Great Depression began, and by 1934 its profits helped offset substantial losses in lumber. The situation rubbed old-time lumbermen the wrong way. "We are lumbermen and must remain lumbermen," wrote Timber Company Vice President and Director A. W. Clapp in 1932. "We cannot allow the tail, even a healthy tail, to wag the dog, even a mangy one."[46] The pulp mill's dependence on raw material from

the lumber and logging operations complicated this. The costs of those materials and mutual equipment such as locomotive engines were often contested.

As the company grew, the financial costs of a lack of coordination became significant. For instance, company sawmills often obtained logs from company logging operations at below-market rates. While the loggers mainly tracked volume, the sawmills were rewarded for profit. Differences in how logs and lumber were taxed after the mid-1940s, however, meant that Weyerhaeuser Timber Company actually lost real dollars to the government that it could have saved by charging the sawmills more for the logs and taking the profit at the logging operations.[47]

Regardless of some growth pains, the company's management won awards. The National Institute of Management named Weyerhaeuser Timber Company "the best managed firm in its industry in the country" in 1954.

The Weyerhaeuser Sales Company was merged into the company's Wood Products organization in 1959, but acquisitions in the late 1950s and 1960s slowed further centralization. Many acquisitions, such as Roddis Plywood, Rilco Laminated Products, and the Kieckhefer businesses, even kept their original names, at least for a time. "There's been an amazing acceptance of all this difference," Steve Hill noted. "In the woods you have a lot of independent people . . . and we have a long thread of autonomous organizations."

During the 1960s and 1970s, Weyerhaeuser used new organizational structures to more closely link different facilities making the same product. There was competition for capital, as well as resistance to implementing improvements developed at other company locations, also known as the "not-invented-here" syndrome. During the slump in the early 1980s, Weyerhaeuser addressed internal competition, redundancies, and inefficiency.

The "organization redesign" of 1982 eliminated overlapping responsibilities and unnecessary layers of supervision. In 1985, businesses were grouped into three organizations: Weyerhaeuser Forest Products Company, Weyerhaeuser Paper Company, and Weyerhaeuser Real Estate Company and Diversified. The changes drew attention to costs, but organizational boundaries remained.

Opposite: Shown in the Columbus, Mississippi, paper mill are (from left) machine operators Diane Nance Howard, David B. Dortch, and George M. Mitchell. Before the mill's lightweight coated paper operations started up in 1982 and again when a new market pulp machine came on line in 1990, thousands of applicants competed to fill the few hundred available job positions.

Construction began on the first Longview mill in 1928, nearly three years after the site's purchase. Inspecting the mill's construction were (from left) sawmill authority and later mill manager Harry Morgan Sr. and Longview's first manager, Al Raught Jr.

45

Starting in 1989, Weyerhaeuser began a refocusing process. Businesses that had formerly been separate, such as the containerboard and corrugated packaging operations, merged to better focus on integrated profits. Businesswide and companywide "best practices" and a single company vision with a newly documented set of values for succeeding as "one company" were developed.

FUTURE OF THE FAMILY

Retired Chief Executive Officer and President Jack Creighton said that operating as "one company" may be among the challenges Weyerhaeuser people face as they enter the 21st century. His successor, Steve Rogel, called further unification one of the critical areas he would emphasize. As Weyerhaeuser people

strive as individuals to accept more diversity, they must be more unified as a team. And membership on that team extends beyond employees to suppliers, shareholders, customers, and the communities where Weyerhaeuser does business.

For employees who might view human values and financial return as mutually exclusive, President Steve Rogel said, "It's my job to show people why that's not true. If you give the shareholder more or the customer more, subtracting from somewhere else isn't the game. The secret lies in earning more." Greater profit benefits all the company's stakeholders: employees, shareholders, customers, suppliers, and the community.

That's the sort of thinking that Weyerhaeuser leaders expect to take the company into the 21st century. It calls for the integration of safety and productivity, diversity and unification, leadership and employee empowerment, family sentiments and financial return. Achieving such integration requires new ways of thinking and of working together. The changes aren't easy. The results show, however, that the more Weyerhaeuser's people are valued, the more valuable they become.

CHAPTER TWO

Doing What We Say We Will Do

Each week, the U.S. Postal Service delivers more than 6,000 envelopes bearing payments for Weyerhaeuser products. In the early 1990s, one of those checks caught the eye of a company accountant in Columbus, Mississippi. She noticed that a Wisconsin pulp customer whose delivery trucks picked up pulp shipments as back haul hadn't taken any allowance for the shipping. In pulp sales, shipping is normally calculated into the price. Checking the records, she realized that the oversight stretched over a year. The accounting staff notified Bruce MacHaffie, Weyerhaeuser's zone manager. The next week, he presented the customer with detailed accounting—and a check for three-quarters of a million dollars. "He was just stunned," MacHaffie said.

The refund was a dramatic example of an honesty and integrity that often are neither practiced nor expected in today's personal and business environment.

People at Weyerhaeuser not only expect ethical behavior; they take it seriously. "Integrity is *the* core value," said David Still, vice president and general manager of the company's Building Materials Distribution business. "We do what we say we're going to do."

Weyerhaeuser began to manufacture pulp at its new Longview mill in 1931. The mill, which cost nearly $3 million, produced 175 tons of pulp per day. Here, pulp is loaded for shipment from Longview.

51

Frederick Weyerhaeuser was 41 years old when this photograph was taken in 1875. He was 66 years old when the Weyerhaeuser Timber Company was formed 25 years later. He worked closely with the new company's management until a serious illness in 1904 restricted his business activities.

Shown is George S. Long at the Everett mill in 1926. By then his title had changed to general manager. When his hiring was approved in February 1900, he was given the title of resident manager, an annual salary of $5,000, and an option to buy up to $100,000 of the company's stock.

FAMILY ETHICS

The value that Weyerhaeuser places on integrity sprang from the company's history as a family organization. In 1976, George Weyerhaeuser, chief executive officer from 1966 to 1991, stood in front of his managers to emphasize that "nothing less than integrity, legality, fairness, and ethical behavior" would be tolerated.[1] After all, he told them, "Our name is on the door."

The name Weyerhaeuser has a reputation for honesty going back more than 100 years. Frederick Weyerhaeuser conducted business on the basis of trust and the value of his word. Throughout his career in the late 1800s, customers paid Frederick Weyerhaeuser's invoices without question, whether or not they could read the English on them.[2] In 1872, a reporter called him "one of the few men not required to put up collateral when he wanted money."[3] He taught his children to never do anything that would discredit the family name.[4]

Over the years, company employees took integrity just as seriously—and personally. General Manager George S. Long was known to have said, "It does not pay to lie—it is the evidence of a weak man."[5] During hard times, he allowed company debtors to delay payments. In the U.S. financial collapse of 1907, for instance, Long accepted notes and clearinghouse certificates from mill owners in payment for Weyerhaeuser Timber Company logs. In 1929, during the Great Depression, he arranged for a competitor to skip a payment owed on a land contract, calling it "the proper thing for us to do."[6] Such business practices sealed the company's reputation for integrity and fair play.

As the company was celebrating its 100th anniversary, Weyerhaeuser employees took pride in the company's attitude toward ethical conduct, which many said matched their personal sense of ethics. "I've never had to make a decision I felt was unethical," said Bill Snyder, manager at Dierks, Arkansas.

"There's never been one iota of doubt in my mind," agreed Carl Jessup, vice president of Southern Timberlands. "We're not going to take shortcuts."

In a world of fierce competition, some might have viewed Weyerhaeuser's high road as a handicap. Weyerhaeuser leaders were convinced, however, that high ethical standards paid off in the long run. "We leave to others the approaches to business which may provide temporary advantage, but at the expense of long-term relationships and future loss," George Weyerhaeuser wrote in the 1988 annual report.

"Sometimes you've missed opportunities because you follow that path instead of where some other people may go," Still said. "But over the years you find out that the high road does pay."

A NAME THAT OPENS DOORS

The Weyerhaeuser name and reputation did open doors. Throughout its history, the company has used the merit of its reputation to tell its story and win public support. Because George S. Long and company spokespeople had been perceived as knowledgeable and honest, representatives of industry and government were willing to listen.

"The job that confronted me for the first 10 years was not a lumberman's job, but a diplomat's," Long said.[7] Even before he knew how much company land had been charred by the 1902 Yacolt Burn, Long began writing letters pushing for passage of fire-protection legislation. Before the end of the decade, he had contributed to the passage of Washington's first forest fire legislation, recommended the state's first fire commissioner, and begun a fire-prevention campaign in public schools. He also helped form the Washington Forest Fire Association and the Western Forestry and Conservation Association, organizations of private timber owners who jointly funded fire patrols.

It took a little longer for Weyerhaeuser to persuade Northwest lawmakers to enact tax policies that would permit companies to retain harvested land for regeneration. Long and other company leaders began explaining the constraints to industry and government assemblies at the 1905 American Forest Congress. "It is a simple mathematical demonstration that it will not pay the lumber corporation to pay taxes and wait for a new crop of trees on cutover lands," Long told a newspaper reporter in 1909—the same year he first declared, "Timber is a crop."[8] Not until 1929 did an Oregon tax measure encourage reforestation. In the meantime, while federal and state forest policies developed, Weyerhaeuser leaders offered their views and supporting data when given the chance.

The 1902 Yacolt Burn in the foothills of Mount St. Helens seared 15,000 acres of Weyerhaeuser's timberland and spurred Long's relentless quest for passage of fire-protection legislation and forest fire prevention education in Washington and Oregon.

53

The same approach worked on less sweeping issues. An April 1977 *Fortune* magazine article by Thomas Griffith, "Weyerhaeuser Gets Set for the 21st Century," described how "Weyerhaeuser's most effective gambit is to supply accurate data to Congressmen and their staffs." Seven years earlier, the company had been one of the first in its industry to open an office in Washington, D.C. From that outpost, Art Smyth, a former forester and raw-materials manager, used his industry knowledge and down-home style to advance the company's reputation for candor. An environmental lobbyist once told a newspaper reporter, "Smyth brings an amiability, which has set the pattern for Weyerhaeuser, whereas so many of the timber types come across as a bunch of table-pounders."[9]

"We're acting in our self-interest, but you can believe us," George Weyerhaeuser told the author of the *Fortune* article. "We don't lie to 'em."

Although the company's veracity and integrity are widely recognized, the Weyerhaeuser name did suffer from a popular suspicion that no one as successful as Frederick Weyerhaeuser could have achieved his wealth by honest means. Much of the doubt can be traced to innuendo and outright errors in a handful of magazine articles early in the century. The company and its founders were characterized as "mysterious" and "money-grubbing" and defamed with spurious allegations of stealing land, defrauding the government, and ravaging the forests.

The charges might have been more damaging if they had been accurate in the simplest of facts, but often they were not.[10] A 1907 article in *Cosmopolitan* magazine, for instance, claimed that Frederick Weyerhaeuser controlled 30 million acres of Northwest forestland, when the company in fact owned approximately 2 million acres. Even Idaho forestlands owned by other founders of Weyerhaeuser Timber Company didn't add more than a half-million acres. The same article called Corporate Secretary Robert McCormick "the man in

Shown at the company's first annual meeting are (standing from left) Horace Rand, William Carson, W. L. McCormick, H. H. Irvine, C. R. Musser, F. C. A. Denkmann, R. M. Weyerhaeuser, and (seated from left) George S. Long, Frederick Weyerhaeuser, F. S. Bell, and P. M. Musser.

Opposite: The result of dedicated lobbying by George S. Long, the Washington Forest Fire Association was formed in 1908. As suggested by this image, there were no logging roads, so pumper trucks were modified for use on railroad tracks. Since coal- or wood-fired locomotives were a significant cause of forest fires, however, rail lines often did provide direct access to fire sites.

55

Left: Shown (from left) are Harry S. Mosebrook, the company's director of public affairs until 1975; U.S. Senator Warren G. Magnuson, who was Washington State's senior senator until 1981; Bernard L. Orell, Weyerhaeuser public affairs vice president until his retirement in 1980; and U.S. Senator Henry M. Jackson, who grew up in sight of Weyerhaeuser's Everett mill.

Clemons Log
Camp #2
C Kinsey Phot 58

Charles H. Ingram worked as general manager of Snoqualmie Falls Lumber Company and later as Weyerhaeuser Timber Company's general manager from 1936 until his retirement in 1956.

charge," when, as noted by a Chicago publication, *The Lumber World,* "everybody who knows anything about the matter at all" knew that position belonged in title and in fact to George S. Long.[11]

Other articles made similar errors in figures, historical transactions, and personal characterizations. In decrying the cutting of trees, even respectable writers of the day occasionally succumbed to allegation. In a 1908 article called "The Slaughter of the Trees," Emerson Hough wrote, "Perhaps the greatest of the lumber kings is Mr. Frederick Weyerhaeuser, who is said to be as honest, personally, as any man, but whose agents in many cases were not."[12] Hough did not back up his charge.

As Weyerhaeuser Timber Company grew, its leaders realized they could not take ethical conduct for granted. Integrity became more difficult to define as thousands of employees brought their own perspectives to decisions. In 1953, Frederick Weyerhaeuser's grandson F. K. Weyerhaeuser, then president of Weyerhaeuser's Sales Company subsidiary, learned that the Everett, Washington, sawmill was manufacturing boards a sixty-fourth of an inch short of American industry standards. The difference— less than half the width of a toothpick— allowed the mill to ship the same product to either export or domestic customers. The alternative was to manage two sets of specifications and inventories.

F. K. Weyerhaeuser told General Manager Charles H. Ingram, "This business of selling something that is not as represented bothers me very much." Although Ingram tried to explain the rationale, he concurred that "we should not misrepresent our product." Thereafter, company mills met both U.S. and overseas standards precisely.[13]

The following year, F. K. Weyerhaeuser ended a speech to Weyerhaeuser Sales Company representatives by stressing, "We believe in telling the truth about our products and our transactions."[14] He already had been preaching the "tradition of square dealing" to sales teams for more than 25 years.[15] Since 1928, the 4-Square® brand had carried the promise of Weyerhaeuser integrity to customers and the public. Such messages were just the beginning. During the 1960s and 1970s, company leaders would struggle to reinforce their commitment to ethics throughout the growing organization.

Weyerhaeuser's expansion into other countries and cultures brought new ethical challenges. International operations presented a full spectrum of business behavior. Canadian ethical standards felt familiar to Weyerhaeuser representatives. The company's joint venture with Kamloops Pulp and Paper began in 1964 after a potential British investor failed to make good on promises to provide technical expertise or funds for the mill. Don Andrews, who would later become vice president of legal affairs for Weyerhaeuser Canada, represented the owners of Kamloops Pulp and Paper in negotiations with potential investors. "By the time Weyerhaeuser became interested, the three [owners] were mighty jumpy," he said. "We went nearly around the world trying to get financial help, and got led down a number of terrible paths." By contrast, he said, the Weyerhaeuser representatives were "good, honest, above-the-table sort of folks that made you comfortable."

Andrews was introduced to Weyerhaeuser General Counsel Dan Smith, and negotiations began. There wasn't time to polish every detail. Kamloops Pulp and Paper's license to harvest pulpwood would lapse if it weren't producing pulp before the end of 1965. "Dan and I tied up a few points in an elevator on a handshake," noted Andrews. "A good deal of that was based on goodwill." Construction began immediately, the machines spun out pulp one month before the deadline, and, Andrews said, "It came out very well indeed."

During the mid-1960s, Weyerhaeuser also became involved in operations throughout the Philippines, Malaysia, Indonesia, the Caribbean, and South Africa. The operations were financial successes, but company employees were thrust into cultures very different from their own.

Norm Johnson, who led the company's forest research in Indonesia, recalled being told that the "only difference between our country and yours is that in our country, the little guy gets some of the graft and corruption." The U.S. Foreign Corrupt Practices Act of 1977 acknowledged that some "special" payments might be acceptable when the purpose is merely to cause something to occur that is legally supposed to happen anyway—such as getting customs approvals for imports on which all appropriate duties have been levied and paid. "We worked hard to keep our Americans from getting involved in that," Johnson said. "We hoped our [local] partners could deal with it."

Weyerhaeuser invested in the Kamloops Pulp and Paper Company in 1964. The mill site was located on the Thompson River in British Columbia, near the town of Kamloops. Shown is the construction in 1972 of the mill's main stack, which lifts steam and mill gases more than 800 feet above the valley floor to alleviate buildup of odorous gases during unfavorable weather and wind conditions.

59

Weyerhaeuser entered a partnership with Indonesian investors during the 1960s. The enterprise sold logs and produced lumber from a variety of tropical hardwoods at a profit, but political unrest and differences in business practices between the stakeholders contributed to the company's sale of its interest and its exit from that lucrative investment and most of its others in Southeast Asia during the 1970s.

Previous pages: Shown is the Kamloops, British Columbia, complex. In 1998 its annual capacity exceeded 108 million board feet of lumber and 450,000 tons of pulp.

By 1975, public reports of improper payments to foreign officials by other American companies overseas prompted George Weyerhaeuser to launch an internal investigation. It revealed no improper activities in North America or Japan except for $200 in illegal political contributions made by employees unaware of the law. In other overseas operations, questionable transactions had indeed occurred. The investigators revealed $1.2 million in "improper payments" made by subsidiaries overseas. Although those payments were on the books, and customary where they took place, the company tried to respond from high ground. It reported the payments to the Securities and Exchange Commission and issued a press release reporting its findings. The board tightened approval processes to ensure compliance with applicable laws, allowing expediting payments only when lawful and when no reasonable alternative existed.

"I am personally determined that this company's 76-year tradition of ethical business practice will not become a victim of our growth," noted George Weyerhaeuser.[16] Within two years of this statement, the company had withdrawn from most of its operations in Southeast Asia. Many factors contributed to the decision: disagreements with local partners over strategy, an inability to rely on investments for the long term, and increasing concern about harvesting tropical forests where laws discouraged regeneration and forest management. Not least was a political environment that required armed guards at some operations. Militant political rebels killed more than a dozen local employees in crew bus ambushes. Another employee was killed in a plane hijacking attempt. Conditions were not consistently this extreme, but the difficulties of maintaining employee security and ethical conduct influenced Weyerhaeuser's exit from the tropics.

ACCUSATIONS AND RESOLUTIONS

During the same period, the company's integrity came under fire back home. Incidents such as the 1972 Watergate break-in and the consumer advocacy of Ralph Nader convinced the public that "political ethics" and "business ethics" were unlikely concepts. During the mid-1970s, Weyerhaeuser found itself the target of federal investigations and a number of class-action and individual lawsuits charging violations of antitrust law.

It wasn't the first time that the forest products industry, including Weyerhaeuser, had faced accusations. Various allegations and a few investigations during the 1920s and 1930s found no evidence of crime, but suspicions didn't fade.[17]

Following amendments to federal antitrust laws, the industry again came under investigation. In 1940, dozens of companies, including Weyerhaeuser Timber Company, were indicted for price-fixing. Along with most of the industry, Weyerhaeuser paid a fine and signed a consent decree that admitted no wrongdoing. Still, in the company history published almost a quarter-century later, the authors wrote, "The shadow of the original indictment hangs over them, and more than one executive now believes the case could have been won had it been fought."[18]

That belief was put to the test as Weyerhaeuser fought antitrust charges brought against it during the 1970s. Although most industry codefendants chose to settle and Weyerhaeuser also settled some suits, the company appealed one case all the way to the Supreme Court. The Supreme Court agreed to hear the case, but before the review, the company and the other two remaining defendants jointly agreed to minimize their financial risk by settling for $35 million.

These challenges underscored an emerging gap between the company's self-image and its public image. In 1976, following its internal investigation, Weyerhaeuser moved to close this gap and restore public confidence through a series of meetings to clarify for employees what constituted ethical business conduct—and what didn't. George Weyerhaeuser also commissioned a Business Conduct Committee, chaired by Dick Lucas, vice president of Weyerhaeuser Far East, to answer questions, interpret policy, recommend solutions and, when necessary, bring concerns to senior managers.

As the 20th century came to a close, Weyerhaeuser's Business Conduct Committee was receiving inquiries about concerns ranging from gifts from suppliers to management practices. Employees could choose to remain anonymous, although George Henson, who led the committee in the 1990s, said the committee received fewer anonymous calls than most similar groups in other companies. Henson noted that the Weyerhaeuser Business Conduct Committee was unique in that it included hourly employees in its membership.

During the late 1990s, one of those members was Omar Gallardo, lead warehouse person at the Fresno, California, building materials distribution center. "Employees mainly come to me for clarification," he said. "The company expects us to follow the highest code of conduct, but often there's no right or wrong answer—it's a judgment call."[19]

Recognizing that difficulty, the Business Conduct Committee made education a key responsibility. New employees received the company's ethics booklet when hired. Managers were asked to periodically hold ethics training and discussion sessions with their teams. Employees everywhere were asked regularly to commit to the company's ethical standards. This emphasis helped Weyerhaeuser earn a 1997 American Business Ethics Award in the "public company" category from the American Society of Chartered Life Underwriters and Chartered Financial Consultants.

J. P. Weyerhaeuser was the son of Frederick Weyerhaeuser and the company's second president (1914-28). He was known to keep a small book in his pocket where he noted the names and family information of employees as he met them during visits to mill and woods operations.

While Weyerhaeuser integrity was both a personal and corporate conviction, it was reinforced by close scrutiny. In 1907 Corporate Secretary McCormick wrote, "There is one great satisfaction to me in our business and that is that we have no loopholes and no questionable proceedings that we are afraid of being unearthed."[20] George Weyerhaeuser Jr. said he believed that his grandfather Phil Weyerhaeuser originated the "standard advice" passed along by his father: "Always be ready to read the headline in the paper about what you just did."

During the company's earliest decades, managers did their best to avoid the spotlight. General Manager Long spoke with typical understatement when he told a competitor that Weyerhaeuser leaders "do not feel very much like passing out to the public very much that might be called publicity."[21] Even in making his annual statements to shareholders, Long produced only a few copies, which he collected at meeting's end.[22] Aware that the company's size subjected it to speculation and rumor, he did his best to mind his own business and help others mind theirs.

Long's philosophy of few words and forthright actions accomplished a great deal. Following Long's death, competitor Mark Reed of the Simpson Logging Company credited him with "the harmonious relationship that existed between the Weyerhaeuser Timber Company and the public." Reed noted, "It is seldom, if ever, that you hear a word of criticism or an unkind remark concerning the organization from the public in general."[23]

Nonetheless, the company's position as an industry leader made it a target of attention. It was "the biggest thing in sight in Washington," acknowledged Phil Weyerhaeuser, who ran the company between 1933 and 1956. "We own a natural resource, and the trees stick up for all who care to see."[24]

The company's visibility increased in 1935, when the death of retired President John P. Weyerhaeuser received nationwide attention. The publicity put ideas in criminal minds, and John's grandson was kidnapped for ransom. George Weyerhaeuser, not quite nine years old, arrived safely back home a week later, and the kidnappers eventually were jailed. The ordeal underscored the drawbacks of being in the public eye. On the other hand, it seemed to demonstrate that the tradition of quietly going about business was no longer practical.

64

Following the death of J. P. Weyerhaeuser in 1935, and subsequent newspaper articles about his wealth, his grandson George Weyerhaeuser was kidnapped and held for ransom. Later, he was released unharmed, and most of the ransom was recovered. Shown is young George Weyerhaeuser meeting the press in the front yard of his Tacoma, Washington, home.

Two years later Phil Weyerhaeuser, George Weyerhaeuser's father and the company's executive vice president, said, "The publicity end of the business is something that we have let go by default for a great many years, and have begun to realize that we made a mistake."[25]

The company began communicating in a new way with the public. Advertisements and speeches, countering public fears of forest extinction, announced, "Timber is a crop!"[26] The film *Trees and Men* was released in 1938.[27] Weyerhaeuser Timber Company produced its first annual report—at least, the first published in a quantity that exceeded seven copies.[28] And the 1941 dedication in Washington State of the Clemons Tree Farm—the first commercial application of sustainable forestry—generated widespread publicity, with Clemons earning recognition as the first certified unit in the American Tree Farm System.

CITIZEN OF THE COMMUNITY

Over the following decade, the company's definition of good citizenship began expanding. The company stepped up to support America's efforts in World War II not only with lumber, as it had during World War I, but also with its fleet of eight ships. Four of the ships steamed off in early 1941 to haul supplies to British troops in North Africa and at the Suez Canal, and the remaining four joined the conflict after the United States formally entered the war. Only six would return; German torpedoes sank the

Potlatch and the *Heffron*. In the meantime, the Weyerhaeuser Steamship Company directed operations of 68 freighters and troop ships for the War Shipping Administration. In company mills, managers scrambled to replace employees who were enlisting in the military. The remaining crews bought war bonds and blacked out mill windows so they could work at night without attracting potential enemy bombers.[29]

The "Timber Is A CROP!" print-media advertising campaign began to appear in 1937.

In 1948, company leaders established the Weyerhaeuser Timber Company Foundation. The nonprofit foundation provided a formal way to help fund the needs of communities where the company did business. Previously, Weyerhaeuser leaders had made charitable contributions mostly from their own pockets, a tradition growing from the social standing of the company's founding families. Before the middle of the century, few companies made charity a corporate concern.

"Our giving dates back to 1902," said Liz Crossman, vice president of the Weyerhaeuser Company Foundation. "The belief in giving back to the community and ensuring the quality of life in those mostly rural communities was valued by this company's leadership from the start."

By the 1930s, Weyerhaeuser Timber Company regularly supported the Tacoma Community Chest on a small scale and occasionally contributed large amounts to help build hospitals or a YMCA.[30] Formal establishment of the foundation marked a new era. Over the next 50 years, the foundation would contribute more than $100 million to community health care, education, and the arts. Its success in achieving its mission of improving the quality of life in communities where Weyerhaeuser is a major presence earned it a place in the Small Town America Hall of Fame in 1988.

Today the foundation concentrates on "enlightened self-interest," or alignment between community needs and company goals. Examples include school improvements, youth programs, environmental awareness, and organizations that increase public understanding of sustainable forestry. More than 90 employee advisory teams recommend local causes to support. "They're the ones who know what's important in their communities," Crossman said.

The foundation has boosted its financial contributions by encouraging employees to volunteer time. In honor of its 50-year anniversary in 1998, the foundation sponsored a program to fund volunteer projects initiated by employees. Weyerhaeuser locations responded with more than 140 projects representing over 125,000 volunteer hours.

GOING PUBLIC

As the company became more active in its communities around the middle of the century, the number of those communities multiplied rapidly. Weyerhaeuser Timber Company became first national, then international, during the 1950s and 1960s. Introducing itself to new neighbors became an important concern. The first national advertising designed to sell the company, rather than its products, began in 1952. It featured forest wildlife and explained

Community contribution campaigns have been part of Weyerhaeuser life since 1900. Shown is a mill contributions committee at a 1957 breakfast meeting in Snoqualmie, Washington.

Opposite: A mixed load of lumber and bombs was common cargo aboard the Nashua Victory *during World War II. Shown are longshore workers loading 1,000-pound bombs at Bangor, Washington.*

In 1996 Weyerhaeuser employees organized a volunteer team to participate in "Paint Tacoma-Pierce Beautiful." The team was assigned a house and provided with supplies and equipment needed to repair and paint the home of a low-income senior citizen living in Weyerhaeuser's first community.

68

a prophecy come true...forests for the future by tree farming

Weyerhaeuser Timber Company

the virtues of sustainable forestry for people and animals alike.[31] Before long, the eagles and deer in the ads would be bolstered by radio broadcasts, more film productions, and television program sponsorship.[32] By the time the Weyerhaeuser Timber Company shortened its name and adopted its current logo in 1959, Weyerhaeuser had become a household name.[33]

Communication worked both ways. *Fortune* magazine noted in 1959, "More than most companies, [Weyerhaeuser] has had to acquire a sense of the public interest and to adjust not only its methods but indeed its whole corporate structure to changing political conditions." Those adjustments included "a policy of frankness which, as [President Phil] Weyerhaeuser once put it, 'would have made the founders of this company shudder.' "[34]

Weyerhaeuser's efforts to be a good neighbor were more than talk. The company opened its forestlands to hunters, created public picnic parks on its land, and staffed those parks with Weyerhaeuser representatives.[35] Manufacturing operations hosted public tours.[36] Finally, the public was invited into another area formerly marked "private"—the ranks of shareholders.

By 1953, the stock held by Weyerhaeuser Timber Company's 16 original investors had been dispersed through successive generations and business transactions to 4,200 shareholders. That figure would quadruple to 18,000 over the next decade. Although Weyerhaeuser shares were available "over the counter" from time to time, there was no formal mechanism for offering shares or determining their market value. "We were one of the three or four largest nonlisted, privately held entities in the United States," George Weyerhaeuser said. "The company had reached the point where there wasn't much chance that you were going to be able to hide under a barrel. It made sense to make it a fully public and fully visible entity."

The company's listing on the New York and Pacific stock exchanges in December 1963 brought Big Board status and about 5,000 new shareholders to Weyerhaeuser. Public listing meant new requirements for disclosing financial information, management decisions, and business developments. "Both good news and bad news must be announced with the same promptness," noted *Weyerhaeuser Magazine* in 1963. The public listing coincided with publication of *Timber and Men*, a history of the company commissioned by Weyerhaeuser in the late 1950s, sponsored by Columbia University, and published in 1963. From its history to its account books, Weyerhaeuser was going public.

Right: Weyerhaeuser learned early on that good community relations should be based on accurate information and education. Lou Work, a Weyerhaeuser forester, explained timberland management to a group of grade-school students from Klamath Falls, Oregon.

What that meant continued to evolve, and it sometimes took time for Weyerhaeuser to prove its good intentions to the public. When the company acquired Dierks Forests in 1969, for instance, Weyerhaeuser stepped up harvesting in its new Arkansas and Oklahoma properties as part of a plan to manage the forests on sustainable cycles. The company's clearcutting techniques were new to the area and "a little unnerving," said forester Kenny White, who joined Weyerhaeuser from Dierks. "We were told we were gonna plant trees back, grow them 25 years or so, and cut them down again," he continued. "I was a graduate forester and I didn't believe that. It was even harder for the community to believe it."

Weyerhaeuser's new neighbors were afraid that the company planned to "cut and run." Local Weyerhaeuser managers tried to be reassuring, making presentations to civic organizations to demonstrate the company's long-term interests. Ultimately, seeing was believing. In 1998, White said, the seedlings he helped plant in the 1970s were nearly as big as the 80-year-old trees they replaced. "There are more trees here now than there were 30 years ago," he said. "Now nobody in the community believes Weyerhaeuser is leaving."

A LICENSE TO OPERATE

Integrity has come to mean more than simply "doing what you say you will do." This virtue counts for little if the public despises or fears what you say you will do. In the company's 1971 annual report, George Weyerhaeuser

acknowledged that "corporations are creatures of the society in which they exist and are increasingly affected by changing priorities of that society." The following year he went further, saying, "There is no doubt at all that the public interest may override our economic objectives in certain areas. That is as it should be; we do business by license of the societies in which we operate."

Weyerhaeuser continued to learn what it took to retain that unwritten license. For years, company leaders made valiant but mostly vain efforts to bring the public to the company's way of seeing hot issues from clearcuts to capitalism. Senior managers met in 1969 with representatives of Students for a Democratic Society after the campus organization protested the company's "exploitive economic imperialism" in Third World countries. During the 1970s and 1980s, Weyerhaeuser doubled its efforts to communicate its position on environmental and land-use issues. Company leaders based their arguments on science, law, and hard facts.

Their data were no match for emotion. The goodwill generated by the concept of "The Tree Growing Company," introduced in 1973, slowly dissipated throughout the 1980s. Confronted by an explosion of environmental regulations, Weyerhaeuser discovered that the public felt the company didn't understand public concerns and didn't share public values. In light of this revelation, company leaders discussed how to salvage their reputation and regain public trust.

"The most important thing we've learned," said Executive Vice President Charley Bingham in 1993, "is that we must listen carefully to the public and embody their values in what we do as a company. Instead of talking, we must do more listening."[37] The following year, Bingham and President Jack Creighton began a series of public "town hall meetings." Thousands of people accepted the invitation to come and discuss whatever was on their minds. Creighton called it "a very ear-opening experience."[38]

"I think people were surprised that we were ready to sit up there and take the hard hits," Bingham told a local business journal. However, he added, "We consider all this a long-term investment."[39]

Later he would explain to employees: "We're a company that operates with the permission of the public. We can't operate for long outside the realm of public values. We need to understand those values and act in concert with them. We have to prove to the public that we're worthy of their trust—not with words, but with actions. Only then will we retain our license to operate."

After 1994, the company continued to hold public meetings to guide business decisions. Several company facilities created ongoing public advisory committees. "The committee acts as our conscience," said Lloyd Steeves. He represented the company on the community team assembled to advise managers of Weyerhaeuser Canada's Grande Prairie, Alberta, operations. "Members ask pointed questions, we engage in frank discussions, and they give us good feedback. It's not always easy, but it's done in a spirit of working together."[40]

Similar committees have guided forest management planning in Saskatchewan and the development of mill emergency response plans in Washington State. Weyerhaeuser teamed up with the public for cooperative research, forest policy planning, education initiatives, and environmental activities. For example, the company asked some of its Northwest neighbors what they most disliked about the looks of a harvested area. Armed with specific responses, Weyerhaeuser engaged landscape architects to

Following pages: The Grande Prairie, Alberta, Canada, complex, shown here in 1997, was acquired in 1992. The mill could annually produce 190 million board feet of lumber and 300,000 air dry metric tons of papergrade and specialty pulps.

71

Weyerhaeuser began conducting "town hall meetings" in 1994 as a means to understand community concerns and address them. Shown is a 1994 meeting held in Seattle, Washington.

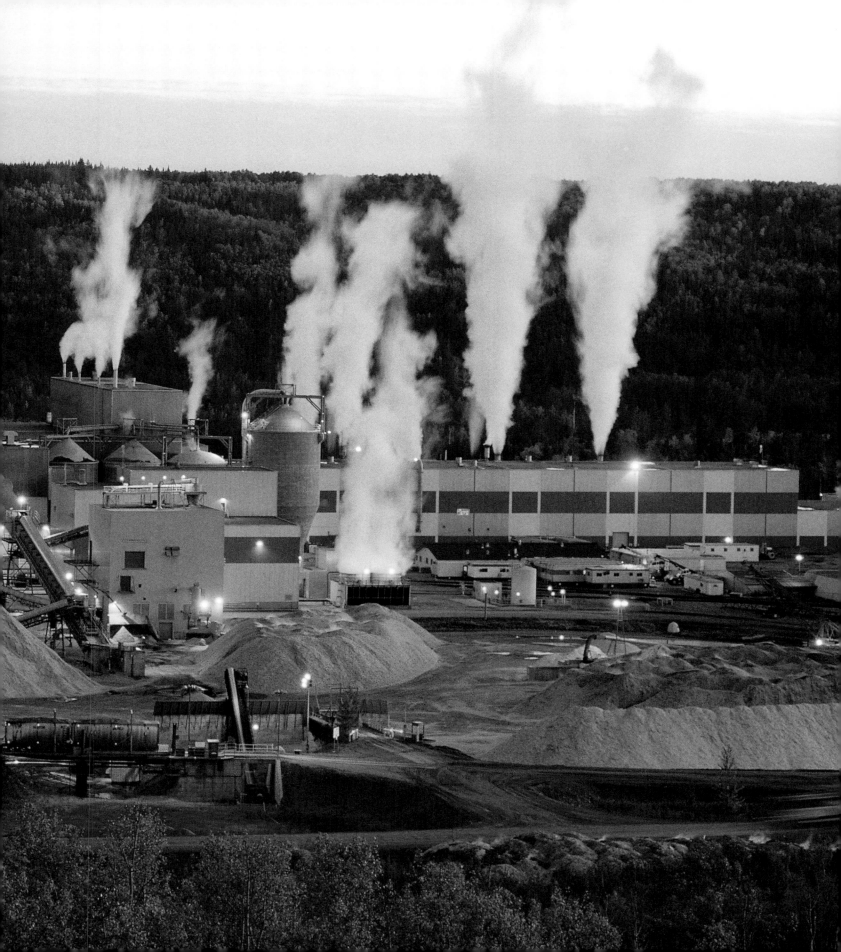

Opposite: Laboratory water-quality testing at NORPAC is necessary to ensure both the quality of its newsprint and the effect of the mill's primary and secondary water-treatment processes. Shown is lab technician Anne Ghosn in 1991.

help plan clearcuts that, for instance, follow natural land contours and leave a line of trees along ridge tops. Public feedback shows that while people still don't like clearcuts, they think the changes do improve their appearance.

INTEGRITY PAYS OFF

In the long run, Weyerhaeuser's citizenship, public accountability, and ethical stance all reflect enlightened self-interest. For three years running, *Fortune* magazine's annual corporate reputation survey placed Weyerhaeuser at the top of its industry in responsibility to the community and environment.

Mike Bickford, director of corporate public relations, said that even the company's former reluctance to communicate wasn't all bad. "That's humility, and that's been a strength," he said. "It adds to our credibility."

"We may not talk too much," agreed George Weyerhaeuser, "but what we say, you can absolutely depend on in intent and execution."

Thus built on performance, the Weyerhaeuser reputation pays off. "The customer is not going to give us much more in the way of pay for a good reputation," said Executive Vice President of Wood Products Bill Corbin, "but we can get in the door. And in the final analysis, all things being equal, the nod will go our way."

David Still offered proof that Weyerhaeuser's reputation means something to customers. A 1988 computer glitch sent duplicate invoices to a long-term customer. When Still apologized—in person—the dismayed customer revealed that to expedite payments, the company automatically processed Weyerhaeuser invoices. The bills weren't even checked against receiving documents or purchase orders. Weyerhaeuser was the only supplier to get such preferred treatment.

Nobody at Weyerhaeuser claims perfection, past or future. Greg Yuckert, vice president of labor relations, put the goal in these words: "We strive to do the right thing."

Weyerhaeuser recognized that doing the right thing required scientific facts. Forestry research expert Dr. Jack Ruffield, at left, and forester Wes Jennings conducted a field study on tree growth.

CHAPTER THREE

Treating Customers as Partners

For some customers, doing business with Weyerhaeuser was the start of a relationship defined by mutual regard and the profitable exchange of raw materials, information, specialty products, or market access. These mutual interests added up to a powerful, albeit informal, partnership. During the 1990s, this premise allowed the company to nurture existing accounts and forge alliances with new customers.

An innovative California company teamed up with Weyerhaeuser to create a specialized wall panel for residential and commercial construction in areas subject to earthquakes and hurricanes. The panels were manufactured using Weyerhaeuser oriented strand board (OSB) and sold through Weyerhaeuser's Building Materials Distribution centers. In 1999 alone, Weyerhaeuser sold more than a million dollars' worth of these wall panels.

So who was the customer, Weyerhaeuser or the panel manufacturer? Since Weyerhaeuser provided both the raw material and the marketing muscle, managers at Weyerhaeuser called it a bookend arrangement. The relationship was established on a foundation of common goals, trust, mutual regard, and shared technology. This approach to customers reflected one of Weyerhaeuser's enduring values. Products changed over the years, but the company's emphasis on partnerships and mutual gain remained constant.

Opposite: Forklift operator Shannon Carrithers moves earthquake and hurricane-resistant wall panels at Weyerhaeuser's Hayward, California, Building Materials Distribution Center. In what was referred to as a "bookend arrangement," Weyerhaeuser sold the finished wall panels manufactured by an innovative California company through its Building Materials Distribution centers in North America.

77

Mile-long trains stacked high with giant logs, such as these shown by the Snoqualmie Falls Lumber Company log pond, were a common sight in the Pacific Northwest during the early 1900s.

Right: These early Everett mill employees lived in an era when many workers made Weyerhaeuser a lifelong career. Pictured after receiving service awards were (from left) George Hammermester, lumber grader, 29 years; Andrew Engblom, lumber grader, 25 years; A.W. Anderson, trimmer, 29 years; Ole Slotten, millwright, 27 years; Henry Kruger, green-chain grader, who started with the company in 1907; Fred Hanich, grader, 20 years; and Olaf Miller, gang sawyer, 23 years. By the end of the 20th century a handful of employees had served the company for 50 years or more, including George Weyerhaeuser, Bob Quick, Marvin Waters, Jake Collins, Roster Lucas, Red Fowler, Phillip Nagao, and Marcia Gleisner.

78

"IF WE MAKE IT, THEY WILL COME"

The company's first customers were small Northwest mill operators. General Manager George S. Long sold them timber partly to reassure them that Weyerhaeuser Timber Company wasn't trying to hoard the supply. In 1900 Frederick Weyerhaeuser instructed Long, "Only sell [timber] at a good profit, as we expect, in the course of time, to manufacture the most of it."[1] The 1902 purchase of the Everett, Washington, sawmill gave company leaders a chance to learn about Douglas fir, a species unfamiliar to the midwesterners, and also provided a close look into Northwest lumber manufacturing and markets.

From the beginning, Weyerhaeuser mills typically made commodity products. Their managers believed that if they manufactured efficiently, the customer would come and the customer would buy. This approach had worked throughout the 1800s for Weyerhaeuser founders, and in the early 1900s there was no reason to change. For the company's first 30 years, Everett and the mills to follow produced softwood lumber products as Weyerhaeuser Timber Company's only business line other than logs and timber.

During this period, market cycles were severe and amplified by weather, bankruptcies, war, and natural disasters such as the San Francisco earthquake in 1906. In years when the economy boomed and construction increased, demand rose and prices were high. The loggers couldn't harvest trees fast enough, and even the biggest locomotives in the Pacific Northwest, pulling trains up to a mile long piled with logs, couldn't keep up with customer demand. Other years, customers could buy lumber cheaply—if they had any money to spend.

Whatever the price, providing a good product was a matter of honor that could earn repeat business. Long believed that satisfying customers depended on attractive prices "coupled up with lumber that pleases him and with service which charms him."[2] Equally important, well-sawn timbers ensured that the company was getting the highest value from each log. In 1915, when the Everett mill manager asked for capital to increase the mill's capacity, Long replied, "I am not so much stuck on making a whole lot of lumber as I am on making it right, grading it right, shipping it right, and doing everything right after the log enters the mill for that is what counts . . ." At about the same time, he began exploring "the idea of having the [Everett] mill adapted to quality cutting in preference to quantity cutting. Possibly a compromise between these two extremes is really what we need."[3]

REACHING OUT TO CUSTOMERS

To make money the company had to keep costs low and increase sales volume. In 1915, Weyerhaeuser Timber Company bought a North Dakota retail lumber business, Thompson Yards. It soon expanded its markets to South Dakota, Minnesota, and Iowa. Weyerhaeuser Sales Company was formed the following year to sell products from 19 mills owned by the Timber Company's founders or associates, including the Timber Company mills in the Pacific Northwest.

Until the formation of the Sales Company, mill sales efforts consisted mostly of handshakes and price lists. Like Long, managers who had

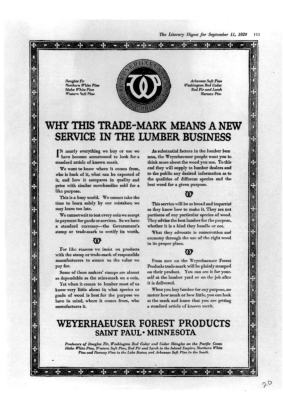

Douglas Fir
Northern White Pine
Idaho White Pine
Western Soft Pine

Arkansas Soft Pine
Washington Red Cedar
Red Fir and Larch
Norway Pine

WHY THIS TRADE-MARK MEANS A NEW SERVICE IN THE LUMBER BUSINESS

WEYERHAEUSER FOREST PRODUCTS
SAINT PAUL · MINNESOTA

Magazine ads, such as this one that appeared in Literary Digest *in September 1920, associated the Weyerhaeuser name with quality.*

begun their careers in sales understood that when prices were equal, lumber was sold on relationships.[4] With the new organization, mill sales representatives who had previously competed to cover the entire Midwest could team up and split the territory among them, becoming familiar with fewer customers and getting to know their needs.

As the Sales organization built closer relationships with customers, in the difficult markets after World War I a joint promotion called Weyerhaeuser Forest Products was launched to promote the products of their various affiliated companies. National advertisements broke with tradition by selling a company name and trademark rather than simply promoting lumber over other materials. The ad headlines read, "Why this trade-mark means a new service in the lumber business."

79

Following page: Weyerhaeuser opened its 73-acre wholesale distribution center in Baltimore, Maryland, in 1922. Its location was within a day's drive of hundreds of eastern lumber dealers. This and two other eastern yards, referred to as Weyerhaeuser's "eastern forests," stocked Douglas fir and other lumber transported by steamship from its Everett and Snoqualmie Falls mills. The Baltimore yard often distributed as much as 40 percent of the Everett mill's annual production.

The ads, which first appeared in the *Saturday Evening Post* in 1920, told consumers that "the Weyerhaeuser people want you to think more about the wood you use. To this end they will supply to lumber dealers and to the public any desired information as to the quality of different species and the best wood for a given purpose. This service will be as broad and impartial as they know how to make it."[5] Before long, the services offered included a house-building booklet and engineers who advised industrial firms such as Studebaker on more efficient use of wood crates.[6] Both the services and the advertising turned retailers into Timber Company partners by building business for those who carried its products.

As retailers took advantage of the Weyerhaeuser trademark, Timber Company lumber became more readily available to customers throughout the eastern United States. The new Panama Canal opened to commercial traffic, and in 1922 the Timber Company opened its first eastern lumberyard, in Baltimore, Maryland. The experiment, profitable from the start, soon expanded to distribution yards in Portsmouth, Rhode Island, and Newark, New Jersey.[7]

To serve these yards, dubbed Weyerhaeuser's "eastern forests," the company entered the ocean shipping business, buying two of the largest World War I freighters afloat in 1923. The maritime operations would later become a subsidiary, the Weyerhaeuser Steamship Company.

When two more steamships joined the fleet in 1925, major shareholder William Carson joked with Long, "If you could raise the price of fir about four dollars a thousand, I would probably advise buying a few flying machines."[8]

4-SQUARE®—AN INDUSTRY FIRST

The company wouldn't get its first airplane for 20 years, but 1925 heralded an even bigger innovation. Carl Hamilton, one of the creative leaders of Weyerhaeuser Forest Products, proposed a radical idea: branded lumber. The company created the 4-Square® brand, combining Weyerhaeuser's "square dealing" reputation with select grades of product cut to exact dimensions, neatly squared on the ends, and protected with a wrapping showing the species, grade, and trademark.

Although most of the Timber Company's directors were enthusiastic, it took three years to put the program in place. Convincing Long was the first step. He was concerned about

The Port of Newark office, shown here in the late 1920s, served as the headquarters for the Weyerhaeuser Timber Company's three eastern distribution yards.

Following pages: Encouraged by the success of the Baltimore Yard, Weyerhaeuser purchased two steamships, the Pomona *and the* Hanley, *in 1923 and opened distribution centers in Portsmouth, Rhode Island, in 1926, and in Newark, New Jersey, the following year. Shown is the* Pomona, *amid other ships contracted by Weyerhaeuser, at the Everett mill wharf.*

The 4-Square brand was created in 1925 as a trademark for Weyerhaeuser's superior-quality lumber products, which were specially trimmed and packaged to be sold at a premium price.

81

Frederick's grandchildren learned the lumber business from the ground up. Shown during their apprenticeships as "fern hoppers" are (from left) Phil Weyerhaeuser and F. K. Weyerhaeuser.

84

"Not room for a thin dime," said Nebraska lumber merchant Jake Kibler as he demonstrated the construction quality possible with 4-Square lumber to Omaha builder Jerry Cery.

confusing consumers and promising a new level of quality, calling it "dangerous to adopt the practice of making an especially good grade for a special purpose." He said, "When you begin to do this you shoot to pieces our regular well-established grades."[9]

Others were certain that 4-Square could be marketed with success. Long agreed to a regional trial. Under Sales Company direction, an engineer designed machinery to handle the 4-Square branding and packaging. The first advertisements appeared in 1928. Mill employees trimmed the new branded lumber to exact lengths so customers could avoid extra sawing. Molding was packaged in cartons. The units were loaded more carefully and covered with paper to protect them from train engine cinders. Those first 4-Square shipments marked the start of a new Weyerhaeuser attitude toward its products. F. K. Weyerhaeuser, president of the Sales Company and eventually of Weyerhaeuser Timber Company, later recalled,

"Our quality was probably no better than the average of the industry—until the institution of the 4-Square program."[10]

The Longview, Washington, mill hired quality-control supervisor Roscoe Howard in 1929 to help ensure the consistent grading on which 4-Square depended. He recalled, "A lumberyard operator once told me, 'I know this Weyerhaeuser lumber. It's sold in hundreds of thousands of feet but it's also sold by the piece to people who only want one board. They will come in and go over my stock, and the Weyerhaeuser lumber is the first that's gone.' The buyer knows that as a general rule, the quality of our lumber is the same today as it was in the last shipment."[11]

Such consistency marked, in the words of F. K. Weyerhaeuser, "a revolutionary change."[12] The revolution wasn't comfortable, however. Mill managers grumbled about slightly short or curved lumber that met grade specifications but couldn't be accommodated by the 4-Square packaging. Even some customers protested. "Species and grade marking are very detrimental to us in handling lumber in competition with others," said Horace Rand, the owner of five lumberyards in Iowa, "and I would not let any of our yards buy regular grade from any mill that was taking out the best of their lumber to make this special grade."[13] Customers like Rand were in the minority. The Sales Company's lumber sales topped a billion board feet for the first time in 1928. Despite the Great Depression, sales stayed over the billion mark through 1930, with 4-Square products leading the way.

4-Square quality was accompanied by special customer services, including construction plans based on standard 4-Square lengths.[14] The Sales Company began offering home construction or remodeling loans, marking Weyerhaeuser's entrance into the home finance industry. "So far as we know, we are the only lumber manufacturer or wholesaler with a finance plan for its customers," noted a 1934 report.[15] As consumers took advantage of these offers, pleased dealers bought 4-Square aprons, caps, and other promotional items. Later F. K. Weyerhaeuser would note with satisfaction "the high degree of preference our branded products are receiving in the market."[16]

The 4-Square brand ran strong for more than three decades. It declined during the late 1960s, after the company's advertising focus shifted to sustainable forestry and tougher markets made customers reluctant to pay a premium for quality. Nonetheless, 4-Square was still in occasional use at the end of the century. Company mills in Canada in 1998 sold a product they called 4-Square Supreme. Russel Kolasa, manager of quality control at the Drayton Valley mill in Alberta, Canada, said that the "supreme" signified lumber that not only was square, straight, and sized accurately but also looked good for markets where appearance was a quality requirement. "It's a visual grade designed for the do-it-yourself retail market," he said.

New products

While Weyerhaeuser product quality was evolving, the products themselves became more diverse. Some products, such as shingles, wooden box parts, and build-it-yourself grain silo kits, were developed to meet customer demand. Many others came about as Weyerhaeuser Timber Company managers worked to get better yield, and thus profit, from each tree.

Since 1917, the company had been involved in the joint research of a By-Products Committee sponsored by the affiliated Weyerhaeuser companies. The products explored included wood chemicals, cattle food, and insulation blankets. The research effort stepped up in 1921, when the Timber Company took 25 percent ownership in the newly incorporated Wood Conversion Company. Its first manufacturing efforts were a wallboard called Nu-Wood and a fluffy

Pulp manufacturing expert and mill manager R. B. Wolf (on left) set high standards for Weyerhaeuser pulp. He developed an early "total quality" management approach to pulp production that included charting production data and painting the mill white to reinforce his insistence on cleanliness.

Right: Shown is engineer William Einzig during construction of Weyerhaeuser's first pulp mill in Longview, Washington, in 1931.

wood fiber product known as Balsam-Wool, which became a very successful home-insulation product.

Another profitable product made from sawmill waste was invented in Idaho at the Clearwater Timber Company in 1929, not long before it merged into Potlatch Forests. Potlatch was owned by Weyerhaeuser family members and other founders of the Timber Company, which obtained a manufacturing license for Pres-to-logs®, a fuel block. The new fireplace logs were also sold as fuel for campers, light-houses, railroad cars, and ocean liners.[17]

INTO THE PULP MARKET

Though popular, fireplace logs alone couldn't consume the mountains of waste generated at company sawmills every day. Hemlock logs contributed even more "worthless" wood until 1929, when Weyerhaeuser Timber Company began building a sulfite pulp mill at Longview. The pulp mill would greatly increase utilization

by consuming hemlock logs that were harvested along with the fir but were not valuable enough to saw into lumber.

The construction must have seemed untimely. To stay afloat through the Great Depression, pulp mill manager R. B. Wolf declared that his team would "make the finest pulp the world knows." He painted the mill white, drilled knots out of the wood being pulped, and insisted on cleanliness to protect the quality of the product, which customers used to make tissue and various other grades of paper.[18]

Half a century before the development of the Total Quality concept, Wolf created a system for measuring and charting product and process variables. Though employees' opinions of "the chartroom" varied, the system contributed to quality consciousness. The proof was in the product. The Institute of Paper

Chemistry used the company's pulp to calibrate testing equipment. John McEwen, an Institute student who would later become a region vice president for Weyerhaeuser, recalled, "That was the thing they used as a standard, because it was so uniform."[19]

To sell its new product, the mill hired its own salespeople, rather than use industry brokers.[20] This break with tradition allowed Weyerhaeuser to form closer ties with customers. The first pulp sales associate, Dave Bigelow, would take potential customers a pulp sample wrapped and tied with a string. "He would knot the string so tight that he could hardly get it off," noted Bigelow's coworker Bob Nash. Bigelow would try to untie it the whole time he was telling the customer about Weyerhaeuser. "He would work on that thing, and he said by the time he got it open, the [customer] would say, 'I wanna see it, I wanna see what you have in that package.' "[21]

By 1933, profits from the pulp mill were offsetting losses from lumber. In 1935 the company announced plans to build a second pulp mill at Everett.[22] Both pulping operations contributed substantially during World War II, when munitions companies began using nitrating pulp, instead of cotton cellulose, for gunpowder.

Nitrating pulp, which was a new product for Weyerhaeuser, may have been the first instance of the company taking on an investment venture in partnership with a customer. Hercules Powder Company paid for half the new equipment needed. Pulp sales manager L. K. "Keve" Larson recalled, "Weyerhaeuser

was skeptical and wasn't going to put out the money, but Hercules was so convinced wood pulp was going to be successful that they put up half." In fact, Weyerhaeuser became the nation's largest contributor of wood pulp for munitions during the war.[23]

There, too, the company earned a reputation for quality. "Not a single pound of our nitrate pulp was rejected by government inspectors," recalled Longview instrument mechanic Herb (Pete) Peterson.[24] Come peacetime, DuPont, Eastman Kodak, and other companies came to Weyerhaeuser for help in making new products such as rayon, cellophane, photographic substrates, and plastics, which were based on dissolving pulps. More traditional customers bought pulp to manufacture paper and tissue. Weyerhaeuser pulp mills had more orders than they could fill.[25]

POSTWAR DEMAND

The company's lumber mills faced their own surges in demand. During World War II, the military consumed lumber as fast as it could be milled. With most of its wood going into Mosquito bombers and Hurricane fighters, the Timber Company tried to support other customers as best it could. While Sales Company employee R. E. Saberson reported partway through the war that "we didn't have a single satisfied customer left in the United States," customers' patriotism generally left them understanding and supportive.[26]

These sheets of Longview pulp were ready to be baled for shipment in the late 1940s. Employees lifted the still-hot sheets of pulp from the cutter box in 100-pound stacks that were pressed into bales weighing 400 pounds each.

87

Following pages: In the 1930s trucks began to replace railroads as Weyerhaeuser's principal means of transporting logs from its forests to its mills, and truck design developed rapidly to meet the new market's demand. Shown is a specially designed diesel-powered Peterbilt loaded with more than 29,000 board feet of Douglas fir—an estimated 233,360-pound load—next to a gas-powered Ford carrying 4,500 board feet.

J. P. "Phil" Weyerhaeuser Jr. served as the company's operating head as executive vice president and president from 1933 to 1956. During his tenure, he helped make quantum gains in log utilization and in product integration at Weyerhaeuser's milling centers.

Right: Researcher Ruth Watts is shown in the Longview pulp laboratory in 1948. The Longview laboratory was responsible for product quality, new process development, and environmental research.

The boom in postwar demand was another matter. Newsletters and training programs for lumber dealers didn't make up for a sometimes embarrassing delivery performance by company mills.[27] Lumber mills traditionally cut each log to yield the highest-value lumber. Unfortunately, that lumber might not be what customers wanted to buy. Orders sometimes arrived months after they'd been promised, in an assortment of grades that bore only a passing resemblance to what had been ordered. By the middle of the century, Weyerhaeuser's reputation for service had suffered.

"Hell, you fellows only want to sell what you want to make, when you have it, whether we need it or not," customers complained to Sales Company district representative Bud Adams.[28] By the mid-1950s, customers who had loyally purchased Weyerhaeuser products for three generations ran out of patience. On breaking the bad news to a Weyerhaeuser sales representative, the owner of a Michigan lumberyard complained, "Old customers never die, they just fade away from Weyerhaeuser."[29]

Adams and his colleagues began writing letters to Timber Company executives. President Phil Weyerhaeuser and General Manager Charles Ingram promptly investigated. The mills complained about sales that didn't reflect their capabilities, while Sales Company representatives pleaded for more timely product information. The Sales Company had become a wholly owned subsidiary of Weyerhaeuser Timber Company in 1948. Its

1959 headquarters relocation to Tacoma helped further eliminate organizational and communication barriers, reducing the friction between production and sales.

RESEARCH AND DEVELOPMENT

In the meantime, the company focused on improving its products and increasing wood utilization. The pulp business created its own research department in 1933 to support pulp production and study other uses for waste wood.[30] More general Timber Company research evolved with the 1942 formation of a Development Department to focus on forestry and utilization research.

In 1958, President F. K. Weyerhaeuser reinforced the commitment to research, saying, "Today, any company which fails to improve its products continuously and to reduce its manufacturing costs cannot hope to attain a place in the forefront of American industry. To meet this need, the company is placing great importance on research and development and product planning."[31] Over the next 20 years, Weyerhaeuser generated innovations in moldable fiber products, laminated beams, and

various composite, laminated, and prefinished panels. By 1978, when the company dedicated a new 450,000-square-foot Technology Center in Federal Way, Washington, Weyerhaeuser was spending $50 million on research each year.

Some new products enjoyed long life spans and solid profits. Others fizzled. "We have been quite ambivalent in the whole question of new product development," acknowledged Norm Johnson, who retired in 1998 as senior vice president of technology. "We have missed the opportunity to stay the course in some of the new things we've done. That's the area I think is our greatest weakness." He pointed out liquid packaging and some engineered wood products as examples of technologies developed by Weyerhaeuser and abandoned, only to become billion-dollar businesses for other companies.

George Weyerhaeuser noted, "Sometimes the first people through [the development process] incur all the headaches and you're better off to be a fast second." The company's process innovations, rather than product inventions, ultimately better served both Weyerhaeuser and its customers. In the mid-1940s, for instance, company researchers invented a way to make Douglas fir chips into bleached white rather than kraft brown pulp. Over the next decade, the innovation became a prototype for mills around the world and helped make the company the largest producer of market pulp in the United States.[32]

The growth in volume was met partly through the development of hydraulic debarking. Although most of the Douglas fir bark already had been removed from the sawmill's wood waste, the whole-log hydraulic debarking technology improved the pulping operations' ability to use whole hemlock logs, increasing the pulp yields from those logs by 25 percent.[33]

Weyerhaeuser worked with a paper-machine manufacturer to develop the extended nip press, which changed the process for making paper to produce higher-strength containerboard. Weyerhaeuser installed the world's first two units in its Springfield, Oregon, mill in the early 1980s. By the late 1990s, hundreds had been installed around the world.

Nowhere was the company's expertise in process innovation more well rewarded than in its most important process—growing the trees that provide its raw material. Formal forestry research began in 1940 as Weyerhaeuser's leaders decided to actively help nature regenerate forests for future wood products. Company foresters first set aside a few stands in which to

The $50 million Weyerhaeuser Technology Center was opened in 1978 to bring together the company's research organizations, facilitate new product and process development, and ensure the quality of existing products.

Whole-log hydraulic debarkers improved pulp yields from hemlock by 25 percent. Shown is a debarker skinning the bark from a Douglas fir at the Longview mill.

92

Opposite: A track-mounted pruning machine is shown working in a southern pine forest near Millport, Alabama. Pruning increases the yield of appearance-grade lumber for molding and plywood.

experiment with thinning the trees. The creation of the Clemons Tree Farm in 1941 expanded the range of experiments to include fire protection, replanting, brush control, and fertilization. Over the next 25 years, this research grew to encompass everything from comprehensive soil studies to forest water quality and wildlife habitat. Genetic research guided Weyerhaeuser's selection and culture of new seedlings, which included cloning technology. The results of the company's first quarter-century of forest research hit critical mass in 1967, when Weyerhaeuser leaders made a commitment to use what the researchers had learned about growing trees faster, straighter, and stronger. Soon all Weyerhaeuser forests were managed under those prescriptions, which became known collectively as High Yield Forestry.

In the last quarter of the century, ongoing forest research at Weyerhaeuser spread to activities as diverse as mapping the locations of owl nests and the development of artificial seeds containing superior tree embryos. Radioactive tracing technology, three-dimensional computer models, and global positioning systems supported forest research by allowing foresters and researchers to project the outcomes of potential forest activities using solid data on growth, wood qualities, and habitat changes.

Spurred partly by its in-depth research into forest health, water quality, and wildlife habitat, the company also has tended to lead its industry in environmental process control, both in the forest and beyond, in the use of its raw materials. Weyerhaeuser technology revolutionized pulp mill pollution control starting in the late 1930s with the invention of a sulfite pulp-mill chemical-recovery system known as the magnesium oxide (MgO) process. In the 1950s, Weyerhaeuser introduced the first vaporsphere to capture and recycle smelly mill gases. In the 1970s, the company created the industry's first mobile aquatic toxicology lab to better study the effects of mill effluent on fish. Environmental concerns about operational and forest management became the focus for much of Weyerhaeuser's research in the last quarter of the century.

Sawmill operation was another area where Weyerhaeuser successfully applied technology. In 1998, surrounded by computer and video monitors, Herschel Janes sat in a control room overlooking the sharp chain rig at the company's Dierks, Arkansas, sawmill. Janes manipulated a joystick and punched buttons as lasers scanned an incoming log and the computer suggested the best way to saw it into lumber. "It pretty much does it by itself," said Janes. "I just manage the flow."

With a view toward the 21st century, technology was being tapped to help Weyerhaeuser manufacture and market the large volume of pruned, second-growth pine that would soon reach harvest size of 18 to 24 inches in diameter in its southern U.S. forests. Bill Corbin, executive vice president of Wood Products, said the coming harvests would offer Weyerhaeuser an opportunity to meet increasing worldwide demand for interior decorative wood products such as windows, in which appearance is the most important characteristic. In addition, Corbin said that emerging technologies for engineered wood products and stress-graded lumber likely would shape future product lines from these forests.

Slow diversification

Earlier in the 20th century, despite commitments to research and the 1930s success of its pulp operations, the company's product lines grew like its trees—relatively slowly. Weyerhaeuser Timber Company took on few new products until mid-century. "We try to conduct our forest enterprises without getting too far into remanufacture or the other fellow's bailiwick," said Phil Weyerhaeuser. He agreed with directors who wanted to avoid making plywood or panel products as long as the Timber Company could sell peeler logs to manufacturers.[34] The company hesitated to breach the line between finding new customers and competing with old ones. Phil Weyerhaeuser's view changed over time.

By 1940, the acquisition of a small plywood and panel business seemed like "a good investment."[35]

Weyerhaeuser bought a majority share of the Washington Veneer Company's single Olympia, Washington, plant in 1940. Although its location and the wood demands of war gave the plant some difficulty in obtaining adequate log supplies, it showed strong profits, and with expertise gained from the acquisition, the company opened a larger plywood plant at Longview in 1947. Washington Veneer was subsequently sold, but another plywood plant began operating at Springfield, Oregon, five years later, while construction began on a Klamath Falls, Oregon, hardboard plant the same year.

After World War II, the company built an integrated facility in Springfield, near its Oregon timber. The new sawmill supplied raw material for kraft-pulping operations, which made linerboard for corrugated boxes, and Weyerhaeuser Timber Company entered the containerboard business in 1949. Virtually all of the mill's initial capacity was contracted to just two customers.[36]

Its 1940 acquisition of Washington Veneer in Olympia helped Weyerhaeuser learn enough about the plywood business to build a plywood plant at its Longview complex. The large new plant, shown here, opened in 1947.

Opposite: Weyerhaeuser began producing containerboard from sawdust and other wood fiber at its Springfield, Oregon, plant in 1949.

95

This logo was introduced at the time of the company's name change in 1959.

▲ Weyerhaeuser

In the early 1960s, Weyerhaeuser acquired the fine-paper mills of the Hamilton Paper Company and the Crocker Burbank Company. Weyerhaeuser's new operations included a 100-year-old former Hamilton mill in Miquon, Pennsylvania, another mill in Plainwell, Michigan, and former Crocker Burbank mills in Fitchburg, Massachusetts, that boasted 20 paper machines.

Amid the postwar economic prosperity, the company also recognized another new customer to be served. It began turning logged land in high-demand areas into recreational second-home developments, kicking off what would become the Weyerhaeuser Real Estate Company.

By the 1950s, Weyerhaeuser Timber Company diversification picked up speed. Over the next two decades, the company took on new customers for bleached paperboard, wood fiber, plywood, veneer, hardboard, paneling, doors, particleboard, paper, folding cartons, and corrugated packaging. The 1960 acquisitions of Roddis Plywood and Rilco Laminated Products launched Weyerhaeuser into hardwood products and nationwide wholesale building materials distribution. By 1962, the company and its subsidiaries made almost 450 different kinds of paper.[37] Given its increasingly diverse portfolio, Weyerhaeuser Timber Company changed its name and logo in 1959 to better express its identity to customers.

"Timber" was dropped and a new, modern logo emphasized green forests and growth. In some of the company's mid-century growth, major customer relationships became business partnerships when Weyerhaeuser customers were acquired and became company subsidiaries. Examples include the 1957 purchase of the Kieckhefer Container and Eddy Paper companies. Before the acquisition, Kieckhefer plants bought almost half of Weyerhaeuser's bleached paperboard and almost one-quarter of its kraft containerboard.[38] The Hamilton and Crocker Burbank paper companies, acquired in the early 1960s, also were major customers of Weyerhaeuser pulp. Such acquisitions made Weyerhaeuser highly integrated, converting almost two-thirds of its own pulp into paper and paperboard, and fashioning three-quarters of its own paperboard into containers.[39] More important, the acquisitions drew Weyerhaeuser out of the Northwest to the southern United States—and beyond.

NEW PLACES, NEW MARKETS

In redefining its traditional markets, the company began looking geographically farther afield. Weyerhaeuser leaders investigated timberlands for sale from Michigan to Peru. The company bought 90,000 acres in Mississippi in 1956, followed by land and mill acquisitions in other southern states. In Mississippi, where the pine timberland initially didn't supply any Weyerhaeuser mill, the company purchased a lumber and plywood mill at Philadelphia in 1967. Other acquisitions and new construction would follow. The Dierks acquisition in 1969 added 1.8 million acres (double the original 1900 purchase) of timberland in Oklahoma and Arkansas along with three sawmills, a kraft pulp and paper mill, a bag and sack plant, two railroads, a gypsum mine, and a wallboard plant.

The company also began building facilities and organizations to serve customers outside North America. The North Bend, Oregon, sawmill opened in 1951 specifically to supply export markets. The ships of the Weyerhaeuser Steamship Company, which became known as the Weyerhaeuser Line in 1962, gradually stopped hauling products from one U.S. coast to the other. Instead, trucks and the company's various short-line railroads transported logs to mills and finished products to domestic customers, while the maritime vessels carried logs, chips, and other products to customers across both the Atlantic and Pacific Oceans.

Nature accelerated Weyerhaeuser's international expansion in 1962, when the Columbus Day storm blew down millions of board feet of trees on 83,000 acres of company land in Washington and Oregon. Like the Yacolt Burn 60 years earlier, and a volcanic eruption 18 years later, the storm forced the company to salvage timber it hadn't planned to harvest for years.

North American markets that year were weak, particularly for the blown-down hemlock. Japanese manufacturers, however, welcomed the white wood. "In export, hemlock was the preferred species and demanded a higher price," noted George Weyerhaeuser, who became executive vice president in 1961.

Shown in 1965 are members of the executive board of directors that led the globalization of the company during the 1950s and 1960s, including, from left, Weyerhaeuser President Norton Clapp, Joseph A. Auchter, Edmund Hayes, John M. Musser, and retired President and Chairman of the Board F. K. Weyerhaeuser.

"So the log trade was a godsend."[40] A Tokyo sales office opened in 1963. By the mid-1960s, the company also had offices and facilities in Europe and Australia and record exports from mills on both North American coasts.

Once the company found those international customers, it naturally wanted to keep them. When salvage logging was complete, Weyerhaeuser began looking for other ways to fulfill the needs of offshore customers, particularly those in Japan. The quest led to

The 1962 Columbus Day storm could have been a financial disaster for Weyerhaeuser. Instead, it prompted the company to find an overlooked market for hemlock in Japan, where the white wood sold well.

Indonesia, Malaysia, and the Philippines, where Weyerhaeuser obtained harvesting rights to more than 2 million acres of timber. Throughout the late 1960s and the 1970s, Weyerhaeuser sold logs and engaged in limited manufacturing in these tropical forests, serving log, lumber, and veneer customers not only in Japan but also in Korea, Taiwan, Australia, and Europe.

"It was demanding and exhilarating because our people were starting up what was, at the time, the largest tropical timber operation ever," noted John Wilkinson, then general manager of Far East operations. During the same period, the company expanded its converting capabilities with joint ventures in paperboard mills and box plants in Belgium, France, Greece, Italy, Spain, South Africa, Jamaica, Guatemala, and Venezuela.

Although the Southeast Asian harvesting operations were well run and profitable, by the late 1970s political, ethical, and environmental forces combined to undermine their viability as a long-term investment. "If you had a half-decent operation, either there were political forces at work trying to take it away from you, or you couldn't enlarge it, or we couldn't apply modern sustainable forestry because we didn't have long-term tenure," noted George Weyerhaeuser. The company decided to withdraw.

Weyerhaeuser's international converting operations also raised doubts during the late 1970s. Few had been especially profitable. "We decided we could serve [international customers] with whatever degree of exports needed and we didn't need the converting operations," said George Weyerhaeuser.

After Ping-Pong matches between the People's Republic of China and the United States during the Nixon era, China sent trade delegations to the United States. Shown (from left) are U.S. Senator Warren G. Magnuson, company President George Weyerhaeuser, and People's Republic Chairman Deng Xiaoping.

Opposite: Log exports across the Pacific began in 1962 following the Columbus Day storm. The newfound markets for hemlock in Japan and other Pacific Rim countries led Weyerhaeuser into what became an important new business.

"So we gradually sold them all off." By 1990, Weyerhaeuser's only operations outside North America were sales offices. Still, the increased overseas business proved to be a rewarding investment over time. The company's exports had grown, making it one of the United States' top exporters, with between 20 and 25 percent of its annual sales to international customers.

Earlier in the 20th century, pulp sales manager Keve Larson had struggled with overseas customers who were reluctant to buy from an American company that might abandon them when domestic markets shifted. "We had to convince our potential customers of the integrity of our intentions to make it a permanent business," he said.[41] By the 1960s, Weyerhaeuser had established itself as a committed long-term supplier to Asian and European companies. Weyerhaeuser was the only U.S. forest products company to be invited to the Canton trade fair when the United States resumed trade relations with China in 1972. Company representatives walked away with an order for 3,300 tons of linerboard from the Springfield mill.[42]

Subsequent business in China took time to develop. According to George Weyerhaeuser, "[Weyerhaeuser Asia president] Bill Franklin and our sales guys in the initial stages did business by going over to the trade fairs. They all stayed in one place in Canton. They'd sit in a room with no furniture for six days and wait to be called to come to talk. You'd wonder if our people were going to be able to survive and be patient enough to worm their way through."[43] It would be 12 years before the company was able to open a Beijing office.

Relations with Japanese customers moved more smoothly. In 1973, after a long courtship, Weyerhaeuser shook hands with Japan's Jujo Paper Company on plans to build a newsprint machine in Longview. The agreement was based on the idea that the two companies could combine strengths to satisfy customers on both sides of the Pacific. Jujo, a major

customer for Weyerhaeuser chips, bleached board, and pulp for newsprint, wanted to expand its newsprint business, but they were interested in a partner and a North American mill site. Because the Japanese newsprint market was dominated by three major producers tied contractually to three major newspapers, Weyerhaeuser had been pondering how to get into the market for several years. "All that came together in a contract which, in effect, melded us into Jujo's supply," said George Weyerhaeuser.

Weyerhaeuser initially owned 90 percent of the new joint venture, known as the North Pacific Paper Corporation (NORPAC). The subsidiary's newsprint machine was constructed in Longview, with half of its 210,000-ton annual capacity committed to Jujo. Two new, specially built vessels chartered by Weyerhaeuser's shipping line, which became known as Westwood Shipping Lines in 1980, transported the newsprint to Japan.

NORPAC produced top-quality newsprint for demanding Japanese newspapers, including the *Yomiuri Shimbun*, the world's largest daily, with a combined circulation of over 28 million. The relationship was so successful that the first newsprint machine had run less than two months before plans for a second machine were drafted. A third started up in 1991, bringing the operation's total capacity to 675,000 metric tons. In 1998 the partnership was restructured to give Jujo (renamed Nippon Paper Industries) a full 50 percent share of the business.

Opposite: NORPAC's first newsprint machine had been producing paper for less than two months in 1979 when the joint venture partners agreed to a build a second machine. Following the completion of machine #2 in 1981, the newsprint operation had an annual capacity of more than 400,000 metric tons, half of which was sold through Weyerhaeuser's Japanese partner, Jujo.

Weyerhaeuser and the Jujo Paper Company agreed to build a newsprint mill at Longview, Washington. The mill was dedicated in August 1979. Shown toasting the joint venture, known as NORPAC, are Jujo President Kozo Toyonaga (on left) and George Weyerhaeuser.

100

Solid relationships with customers and partners like Nippon Paper Industries and the *Yomiuri Shimbun* grew in value for Weyerhaeuser as time passed. "Weyerhaeuser has a presence in Asia at least three times as large as any other non-Asian forest products company," noted Bill Franklin before he retired in 1997 as president of Weyerhaeuser Asia. As the 1970s drew to a close, the company's international customer relationships and reputation provided strength that Weyerhaeuser would draw on during difficulties back home.

SECOND THOUGHTS

Overseas operations weren't the company's only cause for second thoughts during the 1960s and 1970s. Weyerhaeuser reassessed some of its domestic businesses and divested itself of less-profitable paper and paperboard facilities, such as the 33 paper machines in the company's Crocker Hamilton printing and specialty paper operations.

At the same time, however, Weyerhaeuser continued to invest in diverse businesses, partly as a buffer against the cyclical forest products markets. The company's real estate operations grew first with the purchase of residential and commercial land development companies, then with the acquisition of construction companies, and finally with mortgage banking firms and a savings and loan operation. Jack Creighton, who eventually became Weyerhaeuser president, was hired to run the real estate company and, later, the entire diversified business group as it developed. The Shelter Group contributed substantial

income to the company's bottom line, particularly in years when traditional forest products performed poorly. The success fueled additional diversification during the late 1970s and early 1980s.

During the 1970s, the public had come to recognize Weyerhaeuser as "The Tree Growing Company™." For a brief time during the 1980s, the company tried to pursue a much broader base of customers. A revised calling card, "The Tree Growing Company—And More," didn't stick. Though ventures such as salmon ranching, hydroponic lettuce culture, and garden supply stores appeared to be unusual for a forest products company, most weren't unrelated. Salmon ranching, for example, grew from the company's research into warm mill effluents, water quality, fish health, and accelerated growth. Other product lines were extensions of the wood fiber, wood chemicals, and seedling nursery businesses.

As the world's largest producer of market pulp, for instance, Weyerhaeuser supplied pulp to virtually all of the major manufacturers of disposable diapers. In 1970 the company

Despite skepticism, the company established its first nursery at Snoqualmie, Washington, in 1938. Although seedlings were planted in small numbers on company lands in the 1930s, Weyerhaeuser did not begin reforesting routinely with seedlings until the 1950s. In 1999, seven company nurseries raised more than 250 million genetically improved seedlings annually. About half are planted on company land, with the rest sold to other forestland owners worldwide.

Opposite: NORPAC's export newsprint was moved directly from its Longview, Washington, warehouse into the holds of vessels specially constructed for Weyerhaeuser's shipping operations, which became known as Westwood Shipping Lines in 1980. The ships' unique features included covers that allowed cargo to be loaded and unloaded without interference from potentially damaging weather conditions.

103

Weyerhaeuser entered the disposable diaper business in 1970, and by 1988 it was the largest producer of private-label children's and adults' disposable diapers in North America. In 1993 Weyerhaeuser spun off the business.

decided to open its own diaper-manufacturing plants. Over the next 20 years, the company became the nation's largest supplier of private-label diapers, with annual sales of over $300 million in 1990.

Then in the early 1990s, a major technological breakthrough beckoned. Weyerhaeuser bought a process development from Johnson & Johnson and poured millions of dollars into developing its own superior branded diaper. "That turned out to be a gigantic mistake," George Weyerhaeuser said later. Process difficulties, inexperience in consumer marketing, and the sizable investment required to establish brand identity frustrated Weyerhaeuser's efforts. In addition, important pulp customers such as Procter & Gamble and Kimberly-Clark took a dim view of the direct competition. "Jack Creighton and I finally threw in the towel," George Weyerhaeuser said. In 1993, the company spun off its private-label diaper business.

The same year, in the company's largest divestiture ever, Weyerhaeuser found a buyer for its annuity and mutual fund business, Great Northern Insured Annuity (GNA) Corporation. As one of several financial businesses akin to Weyerhaeuser's mortgage banking activities, GNA had been a company subsidiary since 1983. When it grew beyond Weyerhaeuser's desire to keep up with the necessary capital base, the company sold it to General Electric.

The decades of diversification did yield benefits. "Our diversification program that began in the late 1960s and early 1970s . . . has shown its worth," the 1982 annual report stated. "Both Weyerhaeuser Real Estate and Diversified Businesses have shown year-to-year profit improvement despite the recession." That income repeatedly helped boost company profits during especially tough years for forest products. George Weyerhaeuser noted, "Many of the [diversified] businesses that we developed made money and were disposed of profitably."

Meanwhile, the businesses at Weyerhaeuser's heart continued to grow. By 1977, company sawmills processed nearly half a billion cubic feet of logs each year—enough to build a wall 2 feet thick and 15 feet high across the United States.[44] The company had long been the world's largest producer of market pulp. Relatively strong demand for these and other forest products during the 1970s meant that some facility managers routinely started their weeks by reviewing the order commitments they hadn't met the previous week and those they'd likely fail to deliver in the coming week.

Relationships with customers in the company's core businesses were marked by a curious duality. On one hand, customers endured the cavalier attitudes about service that had marked the entire industry since the 1950s. On the other, Weyerhaeuser worked with key customers to provide technical support and other services that extended far beyond normal supplier relationships. Company planes sometimes picked up machine parts, labels, or other materials and delivered them to customers when their other suppliers couldn't arrange timely transportation. Weyerhaeuser helped Fruit Grower's Supply, the distribution arm of Sunkist, build its own box plant, to which Weyerhaeuser would ship raw materials instead of supplying finished boxes. While the teamwork reflected Weyerhaeuser's belief in

customer partnerships, in times of tight supply even close partners sometimes had to accept rough treatment in the form of late shipments, incomplete orders, or marginal quality. Their tolerance would decrease in the stormy markets of the 1980s.

THE QUESTION OF QUALITY

In October 1983, the managers of Weyerhaeuser's corrugated packaging business met to decide how to streamline their organization. The strong markets of the previous decade were gone, and the business had to cut costs. In the midst of the meeting, the managers received a phone call that would alter the course of the entire company. A sales representative relayed a message from an important and long-term customer. The good news: The customer was reducing the number of its packaging suppliers from 17 companies to eight. Weyerhaeuser was number eight. The bad news: Within six months, the customer would eliminate all but the top five. Jim Collett, then vice president of packaging, described the message as a wake-up call. "We think we're good, we know we're the best—but the facts weren't there to support that."

The company plane sometimes served favored Weyerhaeuser customers by making emergency deliveries of crucial machine parts or product components. Starting in the late 1980s, such special services were replaced by a more inclusive and proactive approach to customer satisfaction based on understanding customer needs, customizing product quality, and providing delivery and service beyond industry standards.

Left: Weyerhaeuser entered the corrugated box manufacturing business in 1957, but this did not prohibit it from creating partnerships with paper and paperboard customers that decided to build their own manufacturing facilities. The company helped Fruit Grower's Supply, Sunkist's distribution arm, to build its own box plant in the early 1980s, and thereafter Weyerhaeuser supplied the new plant with containerboard as well as earning additional business for finished boxes.

105

Before applying Charles Deming's Total Quality management principles, the Jackson, Mississippi, packaging plant couldn't turn a profit. Beginning in 1984, however, after employees there started to experiment with the new approach to quality and customer satisfaction, the plant's safety, production volumes, return ratios, and margins gradually improved. Five years later, its profits had tripled.

Opposite: Shown is corrugated container manufacturing at Weyerhaeuser's Portland, Oregon, box plant in 1998.

"We argued with customers," Collett said. "We felt we knew quality and our customers didn't. In the sense of what real quality is, we had a long way to go." Collett said the 1983 phone call began a conversation about quality and doing a better job for customers. He and his team spent the next few years learning from some of the best companies in the world. Industry colleagues in Japan, at the forefront of Total Quality and continuous-improvement philosophies, were happy to help. Packaging business managers brought back a new definition of quality—one that focused on learning what customers wanted, meeting their specifications, and making continuous improvements to increase consistency and lower costs.

Weyerhaeuser employees had thought plenty about quality over the course of the company's history. Total Quality brushed the dust from concepts that had originated with 4-Square—product consistency, reliability, and

extra services that saved costs for the customer. The difference with Total Quality was the emphasis on obtaining the customer's viewpoint and allowing customer needs to drive continuous improvement. "I would say that before, the customer was the last in line," said Tom Luthy, who retired in 1999 as senior vice president of Wood Products. "We were fortunate in that traditionally this is how customers had been treated by the entire segment. Nobody was doing a good job with customers."

Instead of the company's traditional viewpoint, often characterized as "standing in the forest looking out at the markets," Weyerhaeuser began to think about customer needs first—and then about how a wood-based company might fulfill them. This "customer-in" approach contrasted with the company's "product-out" history. Through customer interviews, surveys, focus groups, and crew exchanges, Weyerhaeuser employees learned how strongly customers felt about consistency and timely delivery. Production teams became familiar with the problem-solving and quality-improvement techniques their leaders had brought back from Japan.

The Jackson, Mississippi, packaging plant was among the first locations to put the new knowledge to use. The plant hadn't finished a year in the black since it opened in 1975. In the early 1980s, the operation began listening to customers and involving employee teams in improvement. Safety, production volumes, and margins started to improve. By 1989, Jackson tripled the profits it had earned in 1984.

Employees increased production by 77 percent and slashed the rate of returned goods by 87 percent. On-time delivery went from 89 percent up to 95 percent. This performance and others like it across the packaging business earned Weyerhaeuser the position of No. 1 supplier for the customer who had provided the initial incentive. The success also earned the attention of other Weyerhaeuser business leaders. Total Quality spread across the company.

"We need to have a much, much stronger understanding of—and commitment to—customer requirements," Jack Creighton told employees in 1989. He compared Total Quality to High Yield Forestry, explaining that both involved substantial investments for a long-term payoff. "We have to develop a partnership with our customers, and that takes a lot of time and effort."

Alder is an abundant, fast-growing hardwood that was originally considered best used in home fireplaces as fuel. Weyerhaeuser found, however, that when correctly dried and cut, its white wood was a superior material for manufacturing furniture frames and kitchen cabinets. Shown is Weyerhaeuser's Northwest Hardwoods mill at Longview, Washington.

Sometimes the changes were simple. For instance, the company's Northwest Hardwoods subsidiary created an 800 number for Japanese customers that was answered by service representatives who spoke Japanese. Salespeople began asking customers what more the company could do to enhance those customers' success in the future. Production crews and technical experts visited customer operations to gain firsthand understanding of how the products were used.

Historical tension between sales and production eased as Total Quality concepts changed the company's perspective on what it means to be a customer. "Weyerhaeuser has a good philosophy: We're all customers of each other," said Dino Sordi, a retired maintenance employee at Weyerhaeuser's Kamloops, British Columbia, pulp mill. His words summed up the realization that every employee provided a material or service to an "internal" customer at the next process down the line. Quality and timely performance had to be assured at each step to satisfy the "external" customer.

As Weyerhaeuser employees learned more about their customers, traditional industry standards and specifications were replaced by more stringent customer requirements. A Pennsylvania lumberyard sent back an order of beveled siding in 1988, something the yard had done only twice in many years of business. The yard's owner noted, "The grade we received was the same grade other suppliers were offering, but it wasn't up to the standard we've come to expect from Weyerhaeuser."[45]

When customers' expectations weren't met, Weyerhaeuser managers asked customer representatives to participate in joint improvement teams. One of the tools these teams used was a nine-step problem-solving process that Weyerhaeuser called the Quality Improvement Storyboard. The formal process helped employee teams to use data, not hunches, to close in on the root cause of problems and develop effective solutions. By year-end 1992, more than 140 teams of employees were using similar tools to solve process problems, reduce waste, increase productivity, and improve on-time delivery. Customers noticed the difference.

"It was very obvious that things at Weyerhaeuser were changing," said Dick Gozon, executive vice president of Pulp, Paper and Packaging. Gozon joined Weyerhaeuser in 1994 after more than 20 years with companies that bought Weyerhaeuser paper. "I had kind of a catbird's seat because I was dealing with their major competitors as well," he said. "[Weyerhaeuser] started to become really interested in what the customer has to say, how they felt about their own particular needs. They were taking an interest in quality." In addition, Gozon said, Weyerhaeuser began asking, " 'How can we become better business partners rather than suppliers?' It was a real change."

REFOCUSING

As employees learned what customers really wanted, company leaders began to realize that Weyerhaeuser couldn't satisfy customers—or make money—in businesses in which it could not excel in both quality and cost. "What you forget is you don't have the core competencies to be in some of those businesses," Gozon said. "There's another guy out there who has the core competencies, that's his business, and he'll just kick your butt all over the street." The company's single milk-carton plant, for instance, while profitable, could hardly expect to outdo Tetra Pak, the industry leader with operations in more than a hundred locations worldwide.

The realization helped prompt an effort called "refocusing" that started in 1989. Although it already had eliminated many unrelated businesses, Weyerhaeuser divested itself of another 30 operations that weren't profitable or didn't match its core competencies. In some cases that meant selling businesses, such as its successful gypsum wallboard business, without a strong market share or economies of scale.

As part of its production process, pulp is continually checked for purity and consistency. Shown in 1997 is Glen Murphy inspecting a pulp sample at Grande Prairie, Alberta.

Among other manufacturing endeavors, Weyerhaeuser abandoned milk carton production in 1989 and chose instead to concentrate on its core businesses that were based on the company's principal resource, trees.

The company also stepped away from some customers. Known more for quality and service than rock-bottom prices, Weyerhaeuser operations took a hard look at what they did well and stopped trying to hang on to customers that weren't a good match or that didn't share the company's interest in close, long-term relationships. The Dierks sawmill, for instance, decided to forgo business with most lumber wholesalers so it could focus on supplying wood to truss customers and preservative-treating operations.

"More and more, we're going to deal with a narrow base of preferred customers to whom we're a preferred supplier," George Weyerhaeuser told employees in 1989. Some of those customers made Weyerhaeuser their only supplier. The advantage to Wood Products customers such as Home Depot is that instead of dealing with hundreds of different suppliers, all of the home-improvement store's West Coast locations can be served with the convenience of one order, one set of specifications, and one invoice.

Serving fewer and larger customers applied a lot of pressure to the company's quality efforts. "We have endeavored—and largely succeeded—in getting the strongest customers in the markets we entered," noted Bill Franklin in 1997. "They're often the most difficult to satisfy."

"When you are somebody's sole supply, you really build up close relationships in terms of making sure there are no hiccups in the system and they're getting their [products] on

time," said Scott Marshall, vice president of policy, finance, and strategic planning for Weyerhaeuser Timberlands and Wood Products, "because if they run out, they have no others."

REWARDS

By the end of the company's refocusing, Weyerhaeuser investments in employee education and quality improvement during the 1980s began to pay off. Weyerhaeuser's Winchester Homes subsidiary won one of the first National Housing Quality Awards ever given by the National Association of Home Builders and *Professional Builders* magazine. In 1992, company pulp mills in Plymouth and New Bern, North Carolina; Kamloops, British Columbia; and Columbus, Mississippi, were among the first mills on the continent to earn registration under the International Standards

Winchester Homes, Weyerhaeuser's residential construction company subsidiary in Virginia and Maryland, won the first National Housing Quality Award in 1993.

Opposite: Reminders of Weyerhaeuser's commitment to its customers are visible in all of its manufacturing facilities, including this one in the Marshfield, Wisconsin, door plant.

111

In 1992, the company's pulp mill in Plymouth, North Carolina, became one of four Weyerhaeuser mills to receive International Standards Organization (ISO) certification.

Shown are some of the many publications printed on paper produced by NORPAC in 1998.

Organization's series 9000 quality management standards. Within five years, dozens of the company's pulp, paper, and packaging facilities had achieved ISO 9000 series registration, well ahead of most competitors.

"Some have questioned the role of quality in marketing commodity products," noted the 1990 annual report. The report explained the advantage that Weyerhaeuser's NORPAC mill gained by making newsprint to the quality standards of its Japanese customers, who tend to be more exacting than those in North America. "During the last downturn, our mill was the only one in the West to take no market downtime. In an oversupplied market, customers preferred to order from the top-quality producer."

Weyerhaeuser also renewed its commitment to service. Pardee Construction, one of the company's home-building subsidiaries, developed a new option program for buyers who wanted more choice in the features and finishing details in their homes. The Containerboard Packaging business built a Center for Customer Satisfaction in 1994 to bring together the design, technical, testing, and support resources customers demanded. In the company's timberlands and solid wood operations, employees began to think about "value propositions"—the set of benefits from the products, services, skills, and relationships Weyerhaeuser reliably provides that customers value.

Employees at Weyerhaeuser's hardwood door manufacturing facility in Marshfield, Wisconsin, found a solution in 1995 to its spotty record of on-time and complete delivery of orders. They realized that by accepting "hot" orders and performing last-minute favors for a few customers, they were destroying overall service. They made a risky decision to discontinue hot lists and special favors.

Marshfield's vice president, Jerry Mannigel, said the new policy drove away the plant's largest customer for almost a year. "We had been jumping through all kinds of hoops for them," he said. "When we told them we were no longer going to be doing anything special for them, they thought that meant we were bringing all our customers down to the lowest level of service. Just the opposite happened. Instead we brought everyone up to their level. There's no need for special favors if you meet your commitments."

The new policy helped employees ship customer orders complete and on time 99.8 percent of the time. Even the 0.2 percent of doors not ready to ship on time usually were finished and sent overnight so they arrived on time. Maintaining this 100 percent performance for several years, the plant regained the customer that had left, doubled its output, and increased its market share.

Weyerhaeuser operations began earning preferred supplier awards—and more business—from companies as diverse as Lowe's home-improvement warehouses, Quaker Oats, Gannett Company newspapers, and Xerox. Customers such as Kraft General Foods began signing contractual agreements that guaranteed business to Weyerhaeuser in exchange for ongoing improvements in quality and cost.

FOLLOWING THE CUSTOMERS

During the 1980s, while exports from North America hovered near one-quarter of sales, the company opened offices in Beijing and sold products in more than 60 countries. In 1998 and 1999 a Weyerhaeuser joint venture opened box plants in Shanghai and Wuhan, China, to serve U.S. customers such as Coca-Cola, Anheuser-Busch, Nestle, and others that had

In a joint venture with Swedish-owned SCA Packaging Europe, B.V., Weyerhaeuser opened a state-of-the-art box-manufacturing plant in Shanghai, China. The ceremony included the traditional dragon dance to bring luck, longevity, and power to the new business.

opened operations in China. A Weyerhaeuser box plant in Mexico opened in 1999. "Our fundamental strategy is to follow our customers to serve them better," said Jack Presson, director of business initiatives/international development for the packaging business.

A new generation of international Weyerhaeuser operations eventually will get some of its wood supply from company forests in the Southern Hemisphere. In 1995, Weyerhaeuser announced formation of The World Timberfund, a joint venture that unites the company with institutional investors to purchase international forestlands. Owned half by Weyerhaeuser and managed by Weyerhaeuser Forestlands International, the Timberfund in the late 1990s purchased acreage for reforestation in Uruguay.

"Over the next 20 years the international timberlands will become a significant piece of Weyerhaeuser," said Wood Products' Bill Corbin in 1998. "We learned a lot from having those Indonesian experiences," he observed of the company's previous ventures in international forestry. He said the company was selecting only countries where its business

During the 1990s, Weyerhaeuser Company with a group of investors advised by UBS Brinson formed a joint venture in New Zealand to acquire and manage 193,000 acres of high-production radiata pine forestlands. Shown, from left, in a two-year-old stand of radiata pine are Weyerhaeuser Forestlands International President Conor Boyd; forester Steve Macintosh; and Weyerhaeuser New Zealand, Inc., Managing Director Nick Roberts, who managed the Nelson Forests Joint Venture.

Opposite: Saw line operator Danny Nowesad checked the quality of a newly manufactured sheet of OSB at the Drayton Valley, Alberta, plant.

ethics and sustainable forestry expectations were likely to be met with cooperation and economic success.

"We want to keep up with the growth of customers offshore," said Conor Boyd, president of Weyerhaeuser Forestlands International. "Our customer base is one of Weyerhaeuser's greatest strengths. Unless we grow with target customers, we have to allow others to satisfy their needs. Not many of us have an appetite for that."

PARTNERS FOR THE FUTURE

Entering its second century, Weyerhaeuser would continue to build on its century-long experience with partnerships. The company formed bonds with others that could help it satisfy its customers. Weyerhaeuser called such teamwork "strategic alliances" or "partner relationships." In 1992, for instance, Weyerhaeuser joined forces with a European paper and packaging company, Svenska Cellulosa of Sweden.

The two companies shared technology and process improvements before cooperating to build the two box plants in China.

In 1994 Weyerhaeuser teamed up with SAFCOL, a South African company that supplied softwood logs, lumber, and millwork. What did Weyerhaeuser need with more softwood, particularly as much of its southern U.S. forests matured over the next decade? "We're going to sell what we have plus what we can import," said Ron Van Pool, national sales manager for appearance wood products. The imports allowed Weyerhaeuser to meet customer demand that its own southern forests wouldn't be ready to fill until the next decade. In the meantime, Weyerhaeuser built its customer base. Partners like these accompanied Weyerhaeuser into the 21st century.

Weyerhaeuser CEO Steve Rogel said that this demanded constant innovation and growth. "The biggest challenge is getting this company ready to compete in a new and different world," he said. "In the past we've been better growers of trees and marketers of logs than we have been converters of those logs into value-added products. I knew there was positive change taking place [at Weyerhaeuser] that the rest of the industry had noticed before I set foot in the door. But, customers are demanding ever-better performance in terms of value, and that usually means, 'I want better quality at lower price and faster delivery.' So every year the screw gets tightened another notch."

Member
TREE FARM
American Tree Farm System

®

AFI

owner
Dee Lybrand
—
managed by
Weyerhaeuser

Weyerhaeuser

The Tree Growing Company

CHAPTER FOUR

Stewardship of the Environment

If Tony Melchiors ever handed you a soft drink bottle, you'd need to look before you sipped. Melchiors, a wildlife biologist for Weyerhaeuser in Hot Springs, Arkansas, considered an empty pop bottle a good place to slip a salamander. He sometimes would collect such critters from the woods as part of his research to help Weyerhaeuser manage timberland for all forest residents. "We're counting the songbirds, the rats and mice, and the snakes and salamanders," Melchiors explained.

Understanding wildlife populations is one of the first steps in habitat management planning—a blueprint for providing habitat for endangered species and other wildlife while also accommodating forestry operations. Habitat management planning began during the 1990s as the latest chapter in Weyerhaeuser's long history of environmental stewardship.

The story of that stewardship began in 1900, when Frederick Weyerhaeuser and his partners made their historic purchase of 900,000 acres of forestland in Washington State. In an era when most forest products companies used up their timber supplies and faded within a few decades, the founders planned an enterprise that could sustain itself through future generations. Frederick Weyerhaeuser is credited with marking the purchase by saying, "This is not for us, nor for our children, but for our grandchildren."

The volume of timber on the newly purchased land, while difficult to estimate, was probably in excess of 40 billion board feet.[1] In the company's first 15 years, its only sawmill, at Everett, Washington, shipped less than 75 million board feet per year. Theoretically, it could have sawn the timber then available on

Weyerhaeuser dedicated the first certified Tree Farm in the United States, the Clemons Tree Farm, in 1941. In addition to its own land, Weyerhaeuser managed timberland owned by others, such as Dee Lybrand, who is shown in this photo. By the late 1990s, the company's tree farms covered more than 5.5 million acres in the United States, and Weyerhaeuser managed approximately 35 million acres it owned, leased, or licensed worldwide.

117

company land for more than 500 years before it started on second growth.[2] Even with log and timber sales to other mills, during its first two decades the company harvested at rates that would give it a full rotation of more than 200 years. Nonetheless, as early as 1909, General Manager George S. Long began looking for ways to ensure that there would be "another new crop of timber ready to cut before the old one is gone."[3]

THE BEAUTY OF SUSTAINABLE GROWTH

Since Douglas fir under natural conditions took up to 100 years to grow to harvest size, the two biggest barriers to Long's goal were wildfires and high property taxes. These factors discouraged private landowners from keeping the land after a harvest until a new crop of trees could reach maturity. As a result, U.S.

Prior to the company's commitment to sustained-yield forestry, growing trees was a subject mostly for nature and academics. As early as 1909, Weyerhaeuser began to consider the regeneration of Douglas fir when George S. Long asked the company's cruisers and surveyors to identify possible sites for reforestation experiments.

Forest Service Chief Forester Gifford Pinchot predicted in 1907 that by 1940 the country would face a "timber famine."[4] Long led company and industry fire-protection efforts and lobbied for changes in tax policies to help forestall the "famine."

Convinced that timber could be grown in perpetual cycles, Long asked the employees who "cruised," or surveyed, the company's forests to find tracts suitable for reforestation experiments.[5] The cruisers were happy to oblige. Having spent much of their lives in the woods, many were filled with a spirit akin to that of the era's conservationists. "Many times I have stopped in the woods, alone, and taken my hat off to a fine tree," wrote cruiser Fred Conant.[6]

During World War I, operations managers near Longview, Washington, tried replanting a few acres of harvested land with apple trees.[7] Local farmers weren't impressed; apples grew better elsewhere in the state. In 1922, Weyerhaeuser donated 5,000 acres for Washington State reforestation experiments.[8] The following summer, Long told the U.S. Senate's Select Committee on Reforestation that the company was "exceedingly anxious to get into this reforestation game. We realize the necessity for it very keenly, and out here where the west ends, we want to begin to grow a new forest, and will do it when we have the slight-est chance of making it a possibly profitable enterprise."[9] Long showed the committee why only nature could then afford it: over 22 years, the annual taxes on one 342,000-acre tract had gone from $25,128 to $583,490. Even without considering possible fire losses, such tax increases could well consume future wood values.

Partly on the basis of the Senate committee's findings, Congress passed the Clarke-McNary Act in 1924. As well as expanding the National Forest system, the act encouraged forest-fire protection and changes in state taxation policies.[10] Hopeful, Weyerhaeuser Timber Company directors formed a new subsidiary "to take over, own, control and manage our logged-off land." Weyerhaeuser Timber Company turned over some 200,000 acres to the new subsidiary—the Weyerhaeuser Logged Off Land Company.[11] A few years later Dr. Norman E. Borlaug, Nobel Prize laureate and distinguished professor in International Agriculture at Texas A&M University, observed, "When Weyerhaeuser's management decided to hold and protect logged-off land for regeneration, it was a radical concept."[12]

By 1930, Weyerhaeuser Timber Company had displaced the Northern and Southern Pacific Railroads as the nation's largest private owner of timberland, and tax laws were beginning to change. Charles S. "Chet" Chapman, the company's first full-time professional forester, began developing a reforestation plan that would be in place before logging began near the company's fourth mill operation, at Klamath Falls, Oregon, which opened in late 1929.[13] In an era when company sawmills routinely handled Douglas fir logs 5 feet—and sometimes as much as 12 feet—in diameter,

replacement trees had to grow a long time before the next harvest. A company logging plan developed in the 1930s used a 100-year cycle, with the initial second-growth harvest expected in 2030.[14]

While company leaders such as Long and F. E. Weyerhaeuser were inspired by sustainable-forestry theories, many of Weyerhaeuser Timber Company's old-timers remained skeptical. Charlie Ingram, the company's general manager starting in 1936 and a director until the 1960s, believed through much of his career that when Weyerhaeuser employees started sawing logs that were only as big as could be grown in 80 years, "it would be time to shut her down."[15]

F. E. Weyerhaeuser, the company's fourth president, joined George S. Long as a champion of sustainable forestry.

119

Weyerhaeuser began acquiring Oregon timberlands in 1905. Shown are company directors during a timberland inspection near Klamath Lake in May 1924. The company had already adopted a sustainable-forestry plan for its Oregon timberlands by the time it opened the Klamath Falls sawmill in 1929.

Weyerhaeuser hired Charles S. Chapman in 1924 as its first "scientifically trained" forester.

Opposite: In 1933, J. P. Weyerhaeuser Jr. told company shareholders, "We are . . . committed to the business of growing trees as part of a sustained-yield program." At first the company regenerated its forests primarily by leaving selected trees in each harvested area. In 1949, Weyerhaeuser pioneered the use of helicopters for aerial seeding. Shown is a crew planting nursery-grown seedlings after salvage operations were completed in a fire-damaged forest in Western Washington, a practice that later became part of the company's sustained-yield policy during the 1950s.

Right: In 1925, Weyerhaeuser owned more than 200,000 cutover acres when it incorporated the Weyerhaeuser Logged Off Land Company. Shown (on right) is the company's manager, Alfred "Fred" Firmin, closing a sale of harvested land to buyers who planned to farm it.

120

The appointment of Phil Weyerhaeuser as executive vice president in 1933 marked a turning point for sustainable forestry at Weyerhaeuser Timber Company. The Great Depression actually helped. As part of the National Industrial Recovery Act of 1933 and the Lumber Code that followed in 1934, forest products companies were required to submit plans for restocking harvested land. Of more than 100 companies that submitted such plans, only Weyerhaeuser Timber Company and its subsidiaries or affiliates followed through, leaving seed trees and protecting cutover lands from fire while they regenerated.[16]

Sustained-yield practices made the Logged Off Land Company obsolete, and it was absorbed into Weyerhaeuser Timber Company in 1936. Over its 11-year life it had sold thousands of acres to homesteaders. It now transferred its remaining 150,000 acres to a new Reforestation and Land Department. The same year, Phil Weyerhaeuser announced, "We will hereby be launching on a program of growing trees."[17]

In 1938, the Snoqualmie Falls, Washington, operation created a small seedling nursery.[18] The benefit of replanting was lost on operating managers—and outsiders—who couldn't understand why somebody would want to pay $12 to $15 an acre to plant seedlings when they could go to a tax sale and buy land with 50-year-old trees on it for $4 per acre.[19]

Convinced that sustainable forestry would pay, company foresters and leaders set out, in the words of forester and director C. Davis Weyerhaeuser, "to demonstrate forestry off somewhere apart from any logging operation."[20] They chose 130,000 acres of prime tree-growing land in Grays Harbor County, Washington. Most of the area had been harvested, and repeated fires had prevented all but brush from growing back. Here company researchers started a reforestation project that began as "Operation Rehab" and would soon become known as the Clemons Tree Farm.

Tree farmers

The tree farm idea caught on with the public, and local officials and community organizations expressed their approval for "this great, far-sighted enterprise."[21] A newspaper editorial observed, "At last a start is to be made in practical reforestation. The Weyerhaeuser Company points the way and makes the beginning."[22] The site was named after Charles H. Clemons, a pioneer logger and the owner of the Clemons Logging Company before it became a Weyerhaeuser Timber Company subsidiary.

The Clemons Tree Farm included 130,000 acres of Weyerhaeuser timberland, along with 65,000 acres owned by the state, county, and private landholders. Shown at the 10th anniversary celebration are (from left): Chapin Collins (managing director of the local newspaper), Margaret Clemons (Charles Clemons' widow), Weyerhaeuser Timber Company President J. P. Weyerhaeuser Jr., and former U.S. Forest Service Director Colonel W. B. Greeley.

Previous pages: Shown is second-growth forestland in the foothills of Washington's Mount Rainier.

Opposite: In the 1940s, the company's emergency firefighting arsenal included a network of fire towers where observers lived and worked in near isolation.

Below: Sharpened axes were stored for use in fighting forest fires.

124

The Clemons Tree Farm was formally dedicated on June 12, 1941, receiving official recognition as the first certified American Tree Farm. The event drew Washington Governor Arthur Langlie, who expressed his hope that the tree farm "may set the pace for millions of acres of such lands throughout the state."[23] His speech proved prophetic. Eventually more than 5 million acres in the state would become part of the American Tree Farm System. Within months of the Clemons Tree Farm dedication, other regional and state associations began dedicating tree farms. As the 20th century came to a close, more than 70,000 U.S. Tree Farm members were managing more than 93 million acres of forestland nationwide.[24]

Tree farming ensured the continuity of Weyerhaeuser's own operations, but Steve Anderson, president of the Forest History Society, believes the push to make industrial forestry sustainable also

may have been the company's single greatest contribution to society. "Weyerhaeuser took leadership and had the commitment to forge through the process with the faith that it would be, or would become, profitable," Anderson said.

The first priority at the Clemons Tree Farm was fire protection. Lookouts were constructed with miles of telephone wire strung between them. Three hundred miles of trails and roads crisscrossed the land so tanker trucks could gain access to waterholes to quickly douse any fires. Old-timers laughed at the pumper trucks, but the 24-hour fire crews achieved a 99.9 percent success rate in preventing and controlling fire.[25]

Once fires were brought under control, forest researchers began testing soil-preparation techniques, seed germination, and seedling survival. Most of the company's existing second growth sprouted naturally, but that sometimes took up to seven years. "We were trying to find a substitute for natural regeneration, and we didn't really know how to do it," recalled Ed Heacox, who would eventually become vice president of Timberlands.[26] The researchers experimented with seed distribution and planting tools, then spent evenings lying in the fireweed with flashlights watching field mice devour the day's work.

Aerial seeding techniques proved to be more efficient than natural regeneration. Some would say it was an expensive way to feed mice, but enough seed survived to begin new forests. Still, seeding by plane sometimes left

In 1949, the company began using helicopters to sow seed, control pests, repress weed growth, and fight fires.

Right: Dr. G. H. Rediske conducted tree-growth experiments in 1961 at Weyerhaeuser's Forest Research Laboratory in Centralia, Washington.

"long strips of green seedlings across the hillside with nothing in between," recalled Bill Lawrence, director of forest environmental sciences.[27] Helicopters scattered the seeds better. While company scientists worked to develop seed coatings that rodents would avoid, Weyerhaeuser choppers began sowing up to 20,000 acres a year.

Insect and disease protection, thinning, brush control, the application of nutrients to the soil, and pruning soon joined the list of experimental forest practices. Along with the Clemons Tree Farm, the St. Helens Tree Farm in Washington became a center for Weyerhaeuser forestry research. By the time Margaret Clemons, Charles Clemons' widow, helped celebrate the Clemons Tree Farm's 10th anniversary in 1951, it was clear that growing trees could be profitable.

As techniques for planting, thinning, or other forest management practices were proved at Clemons or other tree farms, they spread through the company. Much of the industry followed Weyerhaeuser's lead. In 1941, U.S. loggers were harvesting 20 percent more timber than nature regenerated each year, and the annual loss from fires totaled 26 million acres. Twenty-five years later, the nation was growing 60 percent more than it harvested, and fire losses had dropped to 4 million acres a year.[28]

Weyerhaeuser began looking for ways to reduce seed loss to rodents and to increase germination rates. "We came to the conclusion by 1950 that there was no real substitute for planting seedlings," Heacox recalled.[29] A program to classify the nearly 400 soil types existing on company lands allowed foresters to choose species and seedlings grown from parent trees thriving in similar conditions.

Seedlings gave the new forest a two- to five-year head start, but they weren't invincible. "We'd put in a whole day of planting, and I'd go out the next day and go over the area that we'd planted and find that the rabbits had eaten 75 percent of the trees," Heacox said. "It was pathetic."[30] Hungry deer, mountain beavers, and pocket gophers also took big bites out of the crop. Although Weyerhaeuser chemists discovered an egg-based repellent that dissuaded deer and elk, damage caused by animals remained a problem for years.

Larger seedlings and sheer volume were better solutions. By 1959, Weyerhaeuser crews planted nearly 10 million seedlings per year.[31] The company still expected the trees to take 80 to 100 years to mature into good sawtimber, however.[32] That time frame wouldn't shrink until the following decade, with the inception of High Yield Forestry.

More trees, faster

Nineteen years after the St. Helens Tree Farm was established, Weyerhaeuser loggers harvested second-growth trees on 135 acres of the Tree Farm. The trees, which had sprouted naturally on land logged three decades before, included plenty of pulpwood and, surprisingly, some trees that in just 30 years had grown large enough to saw into lumber—more proof that timber could be profitably grown as a crop.

The 1962 Columbus Day storm destroyed 130 square miles of mature Douglas fir and hemlock.

In 1961, Phil Weyerhaeuser's son George Weyerhaeuser became executive vice president of Wood Products, Timber, and Lands. By then, the company owned 3.6 million acres of forestland, including nearly a million acres in the southern United States. Joe Brown, the first Weyerhaeuser manager of the company's Plymouth, North Carolina, operations, started questioning the money that the southern foresters were spending to harrow the soil and plant seedlings by hand. "A guy named Harold Nelson spent all winter with a calculator punching out these numbers by hand," Brown recalled. "We spent a lot of time talking . . . and came to the conclusion that it did make sense. It was the first display of the assumptions, costs, and benefits of spending early money."[33]

The report's timing proved fortunate. In 1962, the Pacific Northwest's Columbus Day windstorm blew down 83,000 acres—130 square miles—of trees the company had expected to rely on for decades. Immediately, the amount of wood the company had to

market increased. Once salvage was completed, company leaders had to decide how to sustainably manage what remained, maintain increased production for new export customers, and replace the future forest equity that had been lost. George Weyerhaeuser turned to his foresters and research staff for solutions.

"Grow more trees, faster," they said, an answer that sounded as impossible as it was obvious. Fortunately, the researchers believed that they knew how. In 1966, when George Weyerhaeuser succeeded Norton Clapp as company president, Weyerhaeuser's forest researchers shifted into high gear to prove that intensive forestry would pay off. Using one of the company's first computers, they projected growth from forests under different regeneration, fertilization, and thinning scenarios. Altogether they ran more than 700 computer simulations factoring in dozens of variables.

The result of this number crunching was a theoretical model called the target forest. On paper, the target forest demonstrated that by assisting nature with additional tree planting, thinning, and nutrient application, the company could substantially increase the amount of wood grown on each acre.

Foresters in the South, aided by gentle terrain and backed by a long agricultural tradition, already helped nature sometimes by planting seedlings, controlling surface water, and performing other forest-cultivation

activities. Before 1967, these activities had appeared too difficult and costly to apply in the rugged landscape and heavy undergrowth of Pacific Northwest forests. "It was necessary to make estimates to determine whether 1967 was the time to start bringing intensive forest management to the West," said Vice President of Timberlands Harry Morgan Jr., "or whether we should plan to wait another 20 or 30 years before starting to invest in it."[34]

Since they couldn't predict what products the company might make 25 or 50 years down the road, the researchers abandoned traditional board-foot estimates. Instead, they focused on the tree's basic wood fiber and invented a measure they called a cunit, equal to 100 cubic feet of solid wood. Developing computer programs as they went, the researchers ran projections with the help of Gil Baker, company economist and manager of what became known as High Yield Forestry planning. If reality matched the simulations, the results of intensive forestry would definitely justify the costs. At George Weyerhaeuser's urging, the board of directors approved the High Yield Forestry plan.

Among his other responsibilities as a vice president in the early 1960s, George Weyerhaeuser was in charge of the company's first computer, a large, slow, complicated IBM. When he became Weyerhaeuser's president in 1966, the company's computer was used to develop and analyze the science and economics that supported High Yield Forestry.

Opposite: In the 1960s, as part of its quest to "grow more trees, faster," Weyerhaeuser tested equipment designed for faster, more efficient tree planting, but in its rugged Pacific Northwest forests, the company found that human power was safer and more efficient than mechanical solutions.

129

Following pages: By the 1960s, the economics of forestry dictated a shift from reliance on old-growth harvests, as illustrated in this 1940s Douglas fir logging operation at Weyerhaeuser's Snoqualmie Falls Lumber Company, to the harvesting of small second-growth logs and the manufacture of lumber and other forest products with new high-speed equipment to handle the increasing piece count.

Douglas fir seed cones like these, or cones from other local tree species, are collected at Weyerhaeuser seed orchards in Alabama, Arkansas, Georgia, North Carolina, Oregon, Washington, and Saskatchewan.

Opposite: In the Northwest, High Yield Forestry relied in part on the use of helicopters for distributing nutrients to promote tree growth. In the gentler terrain of the company's southern U.S. forests, fertilizer could be spread by land vehicles.

Right: By the mid-1970s, Weyerhaeuser nurseries had grown, lifted, and packaged more than 100 million seedlings. By the end of the 1980s, the company had planted more than 2 billion seedlings since the 1967 inception of High Yield Forestry. In 1997 alone, Weyerhaeuser nurseries grew 245 million seedlings. Shown is the pine seedling nursery, located in Washington, North Carolina.

High Yield Forestry was launched in 1967, and Weyerhaeuser employees began turning company lands into high-yield forests by analyzing and preparing harvested land. Seedlings up to four years old were hand planted. Over time they were given nutrients, protected from brush overgrowth, and thinned periodically to provide the best trees with the sunlight, space, and nourishment they needed. According to George Weyerhaeuser, the work "captured the attention, the imagination, the vigor—it energized the whole logging and forestry side of our business." The enthusiasm spread. Helicopters and buses carried company leaders and guests to see the new work for themselves.

At first, the company's senior managers were more nervous than excited. "When High Yield Forestry was announced, it was more like a prayer," said George Weyerhaeuser Jr., who accompanied his father to check on the new forests years before he began his own career with the company in 1970. "There had been a lot of research done over more than two decades, but it really was still science as opposed to proven, commercialized practice."

On faith, the company put money behind its scientists' calculations. Before High Yield Forestry, Weyerhaeuser planted a few million seedlings a year. After, the number would reach as high as 200 million. Although the company owned less than 2 percent of the commercial forestland in the United States, by 1976 it performed 16 percent of all U.S. seedling reforestation.[35]

Genetically improving the seedlings proved to be the next frontier for increasing tree growth. In search of a "supertree," Weyerhaeuser established seed orchards using parent trees that had superior growth, straightness, wood density, and resistance to pests and disease. Company nurseries began refining techniques for growing the new trees, including raising some seedlings in small plastic tubes to make them easier to transplant. The combination of genetic selection and better nursery techniques nearly doubled seedling survival rates to more than 90 percent.

Within a decade of its inception, High Yield Forestry was costing Weyerhaeuser more than $80 million a year.[36] It didn't take even that long, however, for the computer projections to become real, thriving forests. By 1975, the company's high-yield forests in the Pacific Northwest were growing more than twice as much wood as unmanaged stands. High Yield Forestry proved even more valuable in warmer climates. The South's gentler terrain lent itself to more mechanized equipment and, years later, more extensive use of such techniques as thinning and pruning, which increased the amount of knot-free wood. As a result,

Weyerhaeuser's intensively managed southern forests yield up to four times more wood than an unmanaged forest.

The full extent of Weyerhaeuser's contributions to intensive forest management remains to be realized. "High Yield Forestry will become increasingly important as we move into the future, recognizing that more wood will have to be produced on a shrinking land base," observed David Thorud, dean of the College of Forest Resources at the University of Washington.[37] John Gordon, Pinchot professor at the Yale University School of Forestry and Environmental Studies, agreed. "As we move toward a world of 10 billion people, what [Weyerhaeuser] and the few like-minded others have done will increasingly be seen to be vital to a brighter future for humankind."[38]

WASTE WATCHERS

While High Yield Forestry increased the wood that Weyerhaeuser could grow on each forest acre, the company also worked on getting more value from each tree. In the interest of creating sustainable operations, employees worked to improve manufacturing efficiency and reduce waste from the company's earliest days.

During the first part of the 20th century, when the trees were enormous, it was economical for the industry to take only the undamaged logs during harvests, leaving any segments of a trunk that contained rot or shattered when it came down. Counting branches, treetops, and stumps, about 80 percent of the tree stayed where it fell.[39] More waste piled up at the mill. Cutting square lumber from round logs left bark, slabs, knotty pieces, planer shavings, chips, and tons of sawdust.

Half the century would pass before increasing wood values and new technology combined to make it profitable and practical to reduce the waste in the woods. In the meantime, Weyerhaeuser worked to make the most of every log it hauled to the mills. One of the first steps was to use waste wood for fuel. The Snoqualmie Falls mill began burning waste wood to generate steam and electricity in 1917.[40] Then new products were developed based on sawmill wastes. In 1929, the company's new box factory at Klamath Falls began converting small or knotty pieces of wood into "box shook," the components of fruit and vegetable crates. Salvage conveyors in the sawmills allowed employees to sort out wood that could be resawn into furniture components or chipped for pulp.

Better utilization of the company's resources meant product diversification as well as significant waste reduction. Early steps included cutting sawmill waste into "box shook" that could be assembled into wooden crates for everything from fruits and vegetables to dynamite and blasting caps.

The development of fiber technology heralded a new way of thinking about the tree. As Phil Weyerhaeuser noted, "In this age of greater utilization, a log is considered a bundle of fibers delivered in an overcoat of bark."[41] Bark and wood fiber research eventually resulted in products for use in molding compounds, adhesives, plastics, insulation, and mulch. The familiar Pres-to-log®, a fireplace fuel developed at Idaho's Clearwater Timber Company during Phil Weyerhaeuser's tenure there, created economic value from what had previously been considered waste.

When the Springfield, Oregon, lumber facility opened in 1949, it was the company's first operation built without the familiar teepee waste burner.[42] It didn't need one. When a log was delivered to the integrated complex, virtually every part of it was put to use.

By this time, new logging techniques such as removing smaller trees before the main harvest helped the company get more wood from each acre. As loggers retrieved more of the wood from the forest, the company's product lines expanded to use it in particleboard, hardboard, and pulp and paper products. Between 1950 and 1975, the volume of products derived from an acre of Weyerhaeuser trees quadrupled.[43] Though the stumps, limbs, and treetops remained in the woods, by 1977 the company estimated it used 98 percent of the tree stem, converting 80 percent to products and generating power from the rest.[44]

Changes in logging practices increased the volume of wood recovered from every acre harvested. The small-log harvesting shown here is a step that takes place before a forest's final commercial harvest. With the development of techniques for small-log harvesting, felling larger trees caused less damage to smaller trees and increased the overall amount of wood recovered per acre.

As fossil-fuel costs skyrocketed during the energy crisis of the 1970s, company operations worked harder to generate more of their own energy from wood residuals. By the mid-1980s, the company had cut its use of fossil fuels in half, reducing air emissions in the process. By the late 1990s, wood residuals (known as hogged fuel) provided about 60 percent of the energy required by the company's large pulp and paper mills.[45] The prospect of even greater energy efficiency prompted Weyerhaeuser's New Bern, North Carolina, pulp mill to start up the world's first commercial application of gasification technology in 1998. When combined with other technologies, the new system was expected to double the production of electricity from mill byproducts while reducing air emissions.

137

Before commercial uses were found for tree bark, chips, and scrap wood, these residuals were incinerated in teepee burners. In 1917 the company began burning wood waste, called hogged fuel, to produce electric power. Shown is the demolition of the Snoqualmie Falls teepee burner in 1976.

Through the years, the company's focus on waste reduction improved the trade-off between economics and pollution control. Employees were reminded that every chemical and every fiber lost as waste was a loss to the company.[46] The company's commitment to clean water and air reached beyond economics and stretched back well before the advent of regulations. For example, in 1906 George S. Long ordered the horse barns of the Maple Valley, Washington, logging operations to be relocated rather than risk contamination of a nearby stream.

When Weyerhaeuser's first pulp operations started up in 1931, the mill took water from the Columbia River to help turn wood chips into pulp, then put the water back along with diluted, used chemicals. The negative effects of this practice weren't necessarily obvious to operators of that era, who sometimes tasted the pulp to decide if it had "cooked" long enough.

138

The company's first research department was established in Longview, Washington, in 1933. Chemist Conrad Becker tested pulp samples there in 1952.

Within two years, however, Weyerhaeuser created a pulp research department to recapture lost materials and preserve water quality. One of the early researchers, Harald Hauff, recalled that their charge was to find "a solution to pollution that isn't dilution."[47]

One solution was to make vanillin from a sulfite pulp byproduct. "The company has a patent for making synthetic vanilla out of sulfite liquor—the 'soup' [left when] lignin and wood fibers are separated. The trouble was, there was a lot of calcium left over; so just making good vanilla did not completely solve our sulfite liquor-disposal problem. Another thing, vanillin from about two [pulp] digesters would supply the whole country for a year."[48]

Hauff and his comrades kept at it. During a meeting one Saturday in 1939, the research team began talking about what happened when various chemicals were burned in combination. Someone suggested that if pulp could be made using magnesium sulfite rather than calcium sulfite, the magnesium sulfite would burn down to magnesium oxide, which could be used again to make the next batch of chemicals. Research director Ray Hatch jumped up to check a chemistry book. An experiment in a 50-gallon barrel led to a patent. After two years of trials and another four years of delay caused by wartime steel shortages, magnesium oxide pulping equipment was installed in Longview in 1946. The process revolutionized sulfite mills and substantially improved discharged water quality.

During the 1950s, the new Springfield, Oregon, pulp mill performed the first large-scale tests of equipment designed to reduce the escape of sulfur dioxide gas. The equipment included surplus World War II barrage balloons, which were used to collect gas from the chip digesters. The balloons were the forerunner of the vaporsphere—a huge steel ball that captured gases so they could be recycled back into mill processes. The innovation revolutionized pollution control across the industry.

A few years later, technicians at the Everett mill developed an air scrubber for the steam stacks. It removed particles such as ordinary sea salt, a ton of which entered the mill every day in logs floated to the mill on Puget Sound. Researcher Jack Murray noted, "Later in 1965 and 1966 when the Clean Air Act came forth, the Environmental Protection Agency used [the air scrubber] as an example of how to meet the pending standards."[49]

By the early 1970s, the company also was ahead of most water-quality regulations, having installed both primary and secondary waste-water treatment systems at every mill. The company's innovations were recognized by others. In both 1961 and 1968, the Springfield pulp mill won awards from the Pacific Northwest Pollution Control Association for air and water pollution control. The association also gave awards to Weyerhaeuser mills at Kamloops, British Columbia, and Cosmopolis, Washington, for industrial water pollution control. Activities at Kamloops and Cosmopolis also earned the company a 1968 gold medal for water-pollution control from the National Sports Foundation.

Efforts by Ray Hatch, a Weyerhaeuser research director, in the 1950s led to the development of what was patented as a vaporsphere, a large steel vessel used to capture sulfur dioxide gas, a pulping process byproduct. Capturing the gas enabled the mill to recycle chemicals and reduce odors.

Awards from the Pacific Northwest Pollution Control Association and the National Sports Foundation recognized the company's attention to air and water quality during the 1960s. Weyerhaeuser had installed both primary and secondary wastewater treatment systems in all of its mills by the early 1970s. Shown along Huckleberry Creek in Washington State is a water-quality team conducting a fish census.

In the early 1960s, public concern about the environment began to grow. In 1962 came publication of Rachel Carson's *Silent Spring*, which stirred environmental concerns that increased over the decade. New understanding and awareness of chemical impacts led Congress to pass federal clean air and water legislation in the mid-1960s. Jo Julson, manager of Springfield's containerboard mill, became the first environmental affairs director in the industry when he was named Weyerhaeuser's director of air and water resources in 1967.

In 1970 the Weyerhaeuser annual report noted, "The nation is entering an environmental era in which ecology is recognized as playing an important role." Just one year later, that role had captured peak position as "the social priority with the greatest implications for Weyerhaeuser today." The growing list of regulations was one factor that prompted creation in 1971 of a corporate environmental department and an environmental policy to help mill operations understand and comply with new laws.

Weyerhaeuser's leadership in sustainable forestry and pollution control gave it a large measure of credibility—and a head start. In a 1970 survey by the Council on Economic Priorities, the company was second among 24 pulp and paper companies for application of pollution-abatement technology to existing mills.[50] The following year, *Business Week* magazine gave the company one of five national Business Citizenship Awards for efforts to improve the environment. "The key to Weyerhaeuser's success," the magazine pointed out, "has been a long-standing campaign, emphasizing research and recycling, to couple environmental protection with production savings."[51]

Those dual objectives came together in 1973 when the company wanted to expand its Plymouth pulp and paper mill. There wasn't enough raw material nearby, so company managers took a second look at used fiber. For many years, Weyerhaeuser's box plants had collected containerboard clippings for recycling by the mills on a small scale. Now "secondary fiber" became an official company business, making Weyerhaeuser one of the nation's first recycling companies. In 1974, a plant opened in Charlotte, North Carolina, to buy and recycle old corrugated containers from supermarkets and other sources. Two years later, another facility opened in North Carolina at a Raleigh landfill to recover even more corrugated material.

"You get the best of both worlds," George Weyerhaeuser said. "We eliminate a portion of the solid waste problem; we stretch the available supply of wood fiber."[52] Starting with less than 25,000 tons per year, Weyerhaeuser's recycling business nearly doubled the amount of recyclable materials it collected every five years, hitting half a million tons in 1982 and 1 million tons in 1987. By the end of the 1990s, the business collected more than 3 million tons

140

Jewell Orvin "Jo" Julson became the first environmental affairs director in the forest products industry when he was appointed Weyerhaeuser's director of air and water resources in 1967.

Opposite: Weyerhaeuser became one of the first paper-recycling companies in the United States when it opened a corrugated container recycling center in Charlotte, North Carolina, in 1974. Later it began to recycle other grades of paper. Shown is the NORPAC facility at Longview, Washington, which processed more than 600 metric tons of old newsprint daily by 1999.

"Best of the S.O.B.s"

article by JOHN G. MITCHELL / photography by EARL ROBERGE

 During the 1970s, many environmental groups recognized the company's successes even as they increasingly raised environmental concerns. The Audubon Society Magazine article in 1974 called Weyerhaeuser the "Best of the SOBs."

of recovered wastepaper annually; nationwide, more than 3 million people participated in the company's office wastepaper collection system, We-cycle Office Wastepaper (WOW).

During the 1970s, even detractors acknowledged Weyerhaeuser's environmental leadership. One conservation writer dubbed the company the "Best of the SOBs." In 1974, the magazine of the National Audubon Society used the backhanded compliment as the title of an article on Weyerhaeuser. Author John Mitchell ended by stating, "Perhaps it is not too late for environmentalists and timbermen to strive for constructive accord."[53]

Yet accord would prove difficult to come by as the Clean Water Act, the Endangered Species Act, and other new legislation affected company operations. By the mid-1970s, Weyerhaeuser began protesting what it viewed as potentially runaway regulations. George

Weyerhaeuser asked in a 1972 interview: "How do you build a plant today that will meet the environmental demands of 10 years from now when you can't even find out what the demands will be a month from now?"[54]

FROM POLLUTION CONTROL TO POLLUTION PREVENTION

Looking for solutions, the company shifted its research focus from pollution control to pollution prevention. "As a company, we believe that basic changes of the manufacturing processes will provide the best solution to environmental cleanup," George Weyerhaeuser wrote in the company's 1975 annual report. The following year, Bill Ruckelshaus joined the company as senior vice president of law and corporate affairs, after having served as the first administrator of the U.S. Environmental Protection Agency. Not coincidentally, the year's report noted Weyerhaeuser's collaborative attempts with others in the industry and in government to shift regulatory emphasis from technologies to results: "To us, the test of regulatory success should not be the amount of hardware applied to the pollution-control effort. It should be, instead, the degree of improvement in water and air quality."

The link between waste reduction and economic improvement continued to reinforce Weyerhaeuser's approach to protecting the environment. An unnamed company executive quoted in a 1977 *Fortune* article said, "Every time we make a forced change, we end up with a benefit."[55] For instance, successful efforts to further reduce pulp-mill emissions of smelly sulfur compounds significantly reduced the company's costs for sulfur. Equipment modernizations designed to achieve environmental goals often increased quality or productivity as well.

Meanwhile, tree planting continued. "Through the lean years and through the good years, we have always spent the money necessary to reforest our lands," said Arkansas forester Kenny White. During the 1970s Weyerhaeuser planted more than a billion seedlings, lending weight to its "The Tree Growing Company™" tag line. The company's forest research group changed its name to "forest environmental sciences" and added experts on wildlife, fisheries, and water. Mike Bickford, director of corporate public relations, who first joined the company in 1973, noted how seriously Weyerhaeuser foresters took their work: "When they walked along a stream or walked through the woods, they were full of pride and passion. They approached their task more like a mission than an eight-hour job."

To a public increasingly concerned about preserving wilderness areas and old-growth forest, Weyerhaeuser helped provide a solution: more wood from well-managed forests allowed more public forestland to be available for other uses. The company readily shared its reforestation experience, making information available to other landowners and providing other tree farmers with advice on improving the productivity and value of their forests.

Bill Franklin (on left), president of Weyerhaeuser Far East, met in 1979 with company representative K. T. Koon (center) and China's Vice Minister of Forestry Zi Gong in Beijing.

The company even helped China start the world's largest reforestation effort. Working with the Chinese Ministry of Forestry beginning in 1979, Weyerhaeuser held seminars for foresters in China, hosted technical exchanges, and provided advice on forest regeneration, nurseries, and planting operations. Bill Franklin, retired president of Weyerhaeuser Far East, recalled: "I'd go to the minister with a consulting contract and there was always something wrong with it, and I finally decided it was an alien concept [in China] to pay for advice. You don't pay your friends for advice—and you only do business with your friends. So we decided we'd give them the help for nothing."

Although there was little industry or academic dispute over the merit of High Yield Forestry, clearcutting practices increasingly came under fire from the public, and some environmental organizations complained that tree farms were not a replacement for "real" forests. George Staebler, director of forest research, later noted, "Ironically, the company was lionized in 1941 for initiating the American Tree Farm movement and ensuring sustainable wood fiber production—and 30 years later, vilified for focusing so heavily on tree farming!"[56] Weyerhaeuser managers emphasized the difference between private forestlands and land owned by the public, but the distinction was not often understood. Regardless of ownership, the public expected to have a larger voice in the management of the forests.

Company leaders recognized that public opinion would play an increasing role in corporate decisions. "There is no doubt at all that the public interest may override our economic objectives in certain areas," noted the 1972 annual report. "That is as it should be; we do business by license of the societies in which we operate." At the same time, supported by ever-increasing demand for wood products, the company held firm to its belief that commercial forestry was not only compatible with environmental protection but also crucial to long-term environmental balance.

Opposite: Ash-encrusted bark had to be cut away before fallers could use chain saws during the salvage harvest of 68,000 acres of prime Weyerhaeuser forestland around the base of Mount St. Helens.

144

Miles of forestland, as well as Spirit Lake, shown in this 1975 photograph of Mount St. Helens, were destroyed when the volcano erupted on May 18, 1980.

THE ERUPTION OF MOUNT ST. HELENS

In 1980, nature again gave Weyerhaeuser an opportunity to prove itself. On Sunday, May 18, Mount St. Helens, in southwestern Washington, erupted. The volcano sits less than 50 miles from the company's Longview facilities and amid 473,000 acres of Weyerhaeuser's oldest and richest Douglas fir forests.

When the mountain's north face exploded, superheated gas swept over more than 200 square miles of hillside, wiping out everything in its path. After vaporizing the nearest forests and flattening more square miles of standing timber, the eruption caused massive floods that swept homes, bridges, equipment, trees, and soil more than 25 miles downstream. Fifty-seven people were killed by the volcanic blast and subsequent destruction.

Company employees were safe, but the blast demolished 68,000 acres—more than 100 square miles—of prime Weyerhaeuser timberland. Charley Bingham, who retired as executive vice president of Timberlands, Raw Materials and External Affairs in 1995, surveyed the destruction by helicopter two days later. "It was just like seeing a thing out of a science fiction movie," he recalled. "Everything was gray. There was no wind. There were no sounds. It was eerie. We flew over one of the steel yarding towers that had been in the area of very intense heat. The yarding tower looked like a sort of oversized corkscrew. It had just melted."

In 1986, George Weyerhaeuser, accompanied by John McMahon, vice president of timberlands, at the St. Helens Tree Farm, set the two-billionth tree to be planted as part of the company's aggressive High Yield Forestry program.

Previous pages: Following the eruption, Weyerhaeuser exchanged 17,000 acres of land within the blast zone for 4,800 acres of government timberland outside what became Mount St. Helens National Volcanic Monument. Replanting of the forests around Mount St. Helens began in 1981 and salvage harvests were completed in 1983. Shown on a late afternoon in 1989 is Mount St. Helens.

In the aftermath of the eruption, the company collaborated with state, federal, and private groups to address safety risks, plan emergency responses, and help turn part of the blast zone into a national monument. Employees began salvaging the millions of Weyerhaeuser trees that had been stripped of their branches and scattered like toothpicks. No one knew if the ash-coated logs could be sawn economically. This was a totally new experience. "The attitude of the senior management and the board of directors was very clear that we would remove every stick of wood and use it where the marginal revenue exceeded marginal cost. It didn't have to make a profit," observed Bingham. "We just don't waste something like that." At peak periods during the next summer, 600 truckloads a day of the ash-coated logs were hauled to mills for processing. The salvage harvests kept the Longview mills busy for nearly three years.

The company's foresters followed the logging crews, delving into uncharted territory: trying to grow a new forest in volcanic ash. Some experts predicted that the land wouldn't recover for decades. Company foresters and forest researchers set out to prove them wrong. Accepting the financial risk of replanting in the blast zone, Weyerhaeuser spent more than $10 million to replant 67 square miles. The balance of the company's forestland in the blast zone became part of the Mount St. Helens National Volcanic Monument.

Six years after the eruption, formal completion of St. Helens Tree Farm reforestation was recognized when George Weyerhaeuser planted the company's two-billionth seedling since the inception of High Yield Forestry. The milestone marked the equivalent of 400,000 trees planted every workday for 20 years.

This historic seedling and 18 million others took root in the blast zone and stunned observers by thriving. Less than 20 years after the blast, the new forest had grown to a height of more than 40 feet. In an area that was once devoid of life, elk and 130 other known wildlife species flourished. In the adjoining national monument, however, the land was nearly barren, and wildflowers and saplings were just beginning to return. The contrast dramatically illustrated both the resilience of the landscape and Weyerhaeuser's capabilities for reforestation.

The decade following the eruption of Mount St. Helens tested Weyerhaeuser's environmental commitment in new ways. "In the forest products industry, the onslaught of the decade following the first Earth Day in 1970 was difficult," said Bingham, "but the general level of prosperity in the industry meant you could afford most of the changes they were insisting upon. The 1980s were just a disaster." Poor markets and low profits meant less money for environmental research or capital investment.

Since the 1970s, the company had invested more than $1 billion to modernize mills, improve quality, increase production volumes, lower production costs, and meet environmental needs. As a result, particulate and chemical emissions dropped by as much as 75 percent. Nonetheless, government agencies applied ever-tighter standards and increased enforcement efforts, and the company was assessed some fines.

The 1985 discovery of minute amounts of dioxin in mill effluents typified the increasing difficulty of manufacturing forest products with due concern for the environment. To understand and control ever-smaller, more elusive air and water pollutants, in 1989 Weyerhaeuser created one of only a dozen laboratories in the nation with equipment sensitive enough to measure dioxin at parts per quadrillion—the equivalent of one second in 32 million years. On the basis of its own research and that of others in the industry, the company began planning nearly $1 billion in capital investments to reduce chemical costs and convert all of its bleached-kraft pulp mills to use chlorine dioxide, rather than elemental chlorine, in its bleaching systems. The changes brought elemental chlorine free (ECF) processes to every Weyerhaeuser pulp mill and reduced dioxin in mill effluents to minute levels below the limit of detection, which in the late 1990s was about 10 parts per quadrillion.

In seeking solutions to other complicated environmental issues, Weyerhaeuser worked with state agencies, conservationists, and other landowners and interest groups. One important collaboration, for instance, was the development of Washington State's landmark Timber, Fish and Wildlife Agreement in 1987. "One of the first things we agreed was, 'Check your weapons at the door.' We're going to go into these discussions trusting each other," recalled

Retired Executive Vice President Charles W. "Charley" Bingham.

149

Shown is a team of Weyerhaeuser biologists conducting an aquatic study near Pe Ell, Washington.

During the late 1980s, Weyerhaeuser and the National Wild Turkey Federation began developing a habitat-management plan to protect wild turkeys and other species in the company's southern forests. In 1995, they signed a partnership agreement aimed at enhancing habitat for wild turkeys and other wildlife and timber production.

Opposite: Weyerhaeuser biologist David G. McHenry collected fish in 1993 as part of a National Pollutant Discharge Elimination System study at New Bern, North Carolina, downriver from the Plymouth mill on the Roanoke River.

150

Destructive black bear habits included debarking Douglas fir to eat the cambium layer, part of the wide-ranging animals' spring diet. Weyerhaeuser established bear-feeding stations to reduce the damage to young forests. During the 1990s, as the company's forestlands grew to more varied ages, animal damage remained manageable.

Dave Mumper, a Weyerhaeuser participant and the director of environmental affairs before he retired in 1998. He said that the agreement's primary benefit was to create a forum and framework for discussing the diverse needs of the state's timber industry, fish, wildlife, water, and Native American tribes.

In the late 1980s and early 1990s Weyerhaeuser generally found success in ensuring sustainable operations through similar cooperative efforts. The company participated with the National Wildlife Federation, universities, and public agencies in research and habitat-management agreements concerning black bears, woodland caribou, wild turkeys,

salmon, and many other wildlife species. In some areas, when it became clear that ecological concerns made intensive forestry impractical, Weyerhaeuser donated or traded hundreds of thousands of acres of forestland to public agencies and conservation groups. In one such swap, the company donated 10,000 acres of wetlands to North Carolina's Great Dismal Swamp wildlife refuge.

As the 1990s arrived, Weyerhaeuser leaders recognized the necessity of expanding the company's long-held environmental ethic. For most of the century, the company had acted on the belief that waste reduction, forest regeneration, and pollution control increased efficiencies and ensured sustainable operations, as well as improved the environment. In the 1990s, public debate and better scientific understanding gave Weyerhaeuser increased perspective on the past—including the company's own mistakes—and on its place in the larger social and ecological system.

"The assumptions of the past don't necessarily work anymore," said Joe Hughes, environmental forester in the company's North Carolina operations. High Yield Forestry principles evolved to maximize wood yield. However, Weyerhaeuser recognized that wood production was not the only important function of a forest, even a privately owned, commercial one. "It means backing off on our long-held practice of maximizing the return from every acre," he explained.

Right: Under the U.S. Endangered Species Act, the northern spotted owl was listed as a threatened species in 1990. This listing necessitated special management of owl habitat, including the establishment of protective zones that restricted logging activity around owl nests.

152

Lupine was one of many wildflowers to revegetate the Mount St. Helens blast zone during the early 1980s.

TAKING A HOLISTIC VIEW

"We're going through an evolution, a transition to looking at broader landscapes and many species," said biologist Melchiors. In the early days, company managers literally couldn't see the forest for the trees. By the close of the 20th century, the company employed an ever-more comprehensive view that considered soil, air, watersheds, animals, and plants, as well as trees and manufacturing operations.

"We're evolving from 'let's be compliant with legislation' to an attitude that says that's a starting point, a C in your scorecard," said John Zagar, corporate environmental manager for Weyerhaeuser Canada.

When the northern spotted owl received "threatened" status under the Endangered Species Act in 1990, the recovery plan included severe restrictions on timber harvests across millions of acres of forest owned by the federal government. Additionally, private landowners, including Weyerhaeuser, had to consider the impact of their forest management activities on the owls. Through its own surveys and government information on spotted owl locations, the company knew it had a large number of spotted owl sites on and near its timberlands, and it carefully planned its activities around each of those sites to help protect the owls.

As it turned out, northern spotted owls weren't as scarce as scientists first thought. Nevertheless, Weyerhaeuser developed exten-

sive protection plans, including a formal habitat-conservation plan for northern spotted owls on more than 200,000 acres of the company's Coos Bay, Oregon, forestlands. The plan provided habitat for the owls while still allowing the company over time to harvest and replant most of its lands. Weyerhaeuser also embarked on an ambitious research program in southwestern Washington to better understand what species of fish and wildlife inhabited managed forests and what impact the company's activities had on them. The company combined the results of the research with a new habitat-management planning process to develop a comprehensive, multispecies habitat-conservation plan for approximately 400,000 acres of timberland in Oregon, as well as a state-based landscape-management plan for approximately 110,000 acres of timberland in southwestern Washington. Efforts on these and other plans continued at the end of the century as the company sought agency approval and worked to implement and improve the plans over the coming years.

This more comprehensive approach to ecosystems also applied to the company's manufacturing operations, where conservation of resources and waste reduction were pushed to the logical conclusion: manufacturing processes that almost completely contained and recycled process materials. The Springfield particleboard mill, for instance, which already used sawmill residuals for raw material, took the dust from sanding and pressed it into new particleboard. Across North America in the late 1990s, Weyerhaeuser pulp and packaging facilities installed water-recycling systems that allowed them to reuse much of their process water, cutting both freshwater consumption and wastewater volumes. As a result, the total volume of pulp mill effluents for each ton of product had dropped by almost 25 percent since 1990 and by 40 percent since 1980.[57] In the intervening years, industry associations and government agencies recognized Weyerhaeuser's efforts and results with a variety of awards for energy efficiency, chemical management, and water-quality improvement.

As the company took a broader perspective on ecosystem management during the 1990s, the number of cooperative environmental efforts in which Weyerhaeuser participated continued to rise. For instance, Weyerhaeuser's Oglethorpe, Georgia, pulp mill was the first facility in the forest products industry to be accepted into the U.S. Environmental Protection Agency's Project XL. The project, a cooperative effort between government and private industry, provided regulatory flexibility in exchange for superior environmental performance. The mill's environmental performance after the 15-year agreement became effective was remarkable. In less than two years, the facility achieved an 11 percent reduction in air emissions and outperformed the EPA's targeted goals by 26 percent for solid waste and more than 30 percent for several key water-quality measures. This performance earned Weyerhaeuser an Environmental Champion award from the EPA and magazine publisher McGraw-Hill.

While cooperative research with universities and state agencies was already a long-standing company tradition, Weyerhaeuser also opened its doors to a wider variety of collaborative relationships and information exchanges. Joint efforts to improve water quality and wildlife habitat often were

153

As early as 1961, honors such as the Industrial Air and Water Protection Award recognized the company's Springfield, Oregon, operations' attention to the environment.

Left: The original Springfield complex, shown here in 1950, manufactured lumber and containerboard. Later, it was expanded to manufacture plywood, particleboard, and ply-veneer.

In 1996, Weyerhaeuser's Oglethorpe, Georgia, pulp mill was the first forest products facility accepted into the U.S. Environmental Protection Agency's Project XL. By 1998 the mill had reduced air emissions by 11 percent and exceeded the agency's goals for solid waste by 26 percent and for several water-quality measures by 30 percent.

Opposite: Shown is the steep White River valley and Weyerhaeuser's White River Tree Farm, established in 1944 in Washington State.

recognized with awards for Weyerhaeuser from civic organizations, industry groups, and state and federal agencies. In the early 1990s, the company began offering community leaders and environmental advocates a firsthand look at its environmental performance. These comprehensive tours through growing forests and manufacturing facilities helped foster dialogue and increase understanding of environmental issues.

That didn't mean that Weyerhaeuser's efforts to build mutual understanding converted everyone to its viewpoint. "It has and always will be an adversarial relationship," maintained the National Audubon Society's Brock Evans in a 1993 article in *Barron's*.

"Even so, the Weyerhaeuser people are friendly, approachable and accessible."[58] Two years later, Alan Copsey of the Washington Environmental Council told *Business Week*, "They're never going to do everything environmentalists wish; if they did, they'd go broke. But they're one of the best at taking care of the land."[59]

Weyerhaeuser's practical and willing dialogue earned praise from the Willapa Alliance, which has been described as a bridge between community, environmental, and business interests in southwestern Washington's Willapa River watershed. Dan'l Markham, the alliance's director of development and former executive director, said, "I don't know how Weyerhaeuser works in other watersheds, but here they have been the most progressive player in the industry. They've been willing to grapple and work on some very difficult issues, including fisheries restoration, with us. They have their objectives and that's fine. We don't care what their motivation is—we're just glad they're doing it."

In a further example of environmental collaboration, Weyerhaeuser joined a "conservation partnership" with the Environmental Defense Fund (EDF) and several other environmental organizations, including the Sierra Club and the National Audubon Society. The partnership involved company land in North Carolina known as the Parker Tract, the last remnant of the East Dismal Swamp.

In the early 1990s, a consortium of environmental organizations sued to preserve this hardwood forest. As part of the resolution of the lawsuit, the company and the EDF agreed to jointly develop a management plan to protect the Parker Tract's ecological values and still allow the company to achieve an acceptable financial return from its forestland. The discussions took 18 months. "There were times when we both thought we would not make it through," said Jane Preyer, director of the EDF's North Carolina office. "We hit some stalemates. We had to break the barrier of whether each group had hidden agendas and begin to get down to 'what do we each really want to achieve?' It took us a while to get there, but it was absolutely worth it."

In 1997, the partners agreed on a management plan for several thousand acres of natural hardwood forest, some that would be virtually undisturbed. The plan protected habitat for black bears, migratory birds, and some rare hardwood trees and swamp plants. The company also would grow and harvest pine on most of the tract, and the partners would study and monitor the area in the coming decades. Both sides called the partnership a model for finding cooperative solutions to tough environmental problems.

Rex McCullough, vice president for Forestry Research, said that at Weyerhaeuser, "We go out of our way trying to do the right thing." The construction of a new company landfill illustrated his point. In the early 1990s, the 60-year-old Longview complex began running out of space for process wastes such as boiler ash and wastewater-treatment sludge. The company built a new landfill on forested land it owned nearby, despite resistance from area residents. "We'd explain that all current regulations require us to do is dig a hole and put the waste in," said Cal Palmer, the company's manager of integrated waste management, as the landfill was built. "But we're putting in liners, we're collecting leachate, and we're meeting or exceeding all federal, state, and local standards. Then the skeptics would say, 'Why are you doing all that unless you're planning to put in something that's deadly toxic?'" Palmer related with a sigh. "All we can do is be consistent and prove over time that there are no harmful effects."[60]

During the 1990s the company offered tours of its forest and mill operations to community leaders and environmentalists in an effort to inform them about how the company tended its land and trees, manufactured its forest products, and protected flora, fauna, and air and water quality. Shown at left is Byron Rickert addressing a tour group in 1996.

Opposite: After 18 months of negotiations, in 1997 Weyerhaeuser and the Environmental Defense Fund announced a joint conservation plan for managing the Parker Tract, a relatively undisturbed portion of the East Dismal Swamp in North Carolina. The company would grow and harvest pine on most of the land, but it agreed to protect several thousand acres of natural hardwood forest for black bears, migratory birds, and rare swamp plants.

157

Shown is a tree-growing experiment at the Weyerhaeuser Technology Center.

Opposite: New technology increased Weyerhaeuser wood utilization by measuring log curvature and using computer-guided blades to literally cut straight lumber from curved logs. Shown is a typical curved pine log, displayed by Tom Harrison, at Dierks, Arkansas.

"The expectations today, when you talk about environmental stewardship, are very different than they were 50 years ago," said retired Chief Executive Officer Jack Creighton. To meet those changing expectations, the company has relied on technology, innovation, and continuous improvement. "A mill operator today would hardly recognize the equipment in our mills 50 years ago," said Dick Erickson, vice president of Environment, Health and Safety. "As we've closed up our processes to eliminate waste, we've gone to entirely new equipment and systems—and we can expect the same magnitude of technology change in the future."

Yet the basic attitude with which company leaders approached environmental challenges only grew stronger with time. The stewardship ethic that prompted George S. Long to keep logged land to be reforested continued to motivate Weyerhaeuser decades later in the 1990s, when the company helped promote the American Forest and Paper Association's Sustainable Forestry Initiative™ and other voluntary industry efforts to encourage sustainable forestry practices.

At the same time, Weyerhaeuser's commitment to sustainability evolved over the century to acknowledge the value of partnerships, as in 1996, when the company played a leading role in the Seventh American Forest Congress. The event attracted nearly 1,500 foresters, environmentalists, government representatives, and labor leaders, who came together to begin reaching agreement on how to use and conserve America's forests.

Charley Bingham, one of the Weyerhaeuser participants, said, "One thing we learned was that people who are interested in the forest from every point of view agree on much more than they disagree. Get them together in a situation where they can talk candidly," he said, and "you'd be surprised what can be accomplished."

CHAPTER FIVE

Stewardship of the Investment

During the 20th century, as the economy and lifestyles changed in the United States, so did many businesses. Buggy makers gave way to auto makers, home-cooked meals to fast-food restaurants, typewriters to computers. The forest products industry saw its share of change, too, yet Weyerhaeuser remained steady in its strong asset base and its conservative approach to finances.

As Weyerhaeuser celebrated its 100th anniversary, its investor base had increased from the original 11 families to more than 25,000 shareholders of record. The company's original forestland holdings of 900,000 acres had grown to millions of acres, annual sales were in the billions, and the company's equity market capitalization was more than $14 billion.

Weyerhaeuser leaders helped achieve this growth by navigating the company through many business cycles, staying focused on long-term horizons. The business principle that guided them was simple: create long-term value for shareholders.

INVESTING WITH AN EYE TO THE FUTURE

In 1900 Weyerhaeuser Timber Company was part of an industry in which companies weren't expected to last. In the early part of the 20th century, many logging and lumber companies were organized around specific tracts of timberland, and those companies didn't survive more than a few decades, long enough to harvest the land and close their mills.

Opposite: Shown is a portion of Weyerhaeuser's Columbus, Mississippi, pulp and paper complex, which was one of the last pulp and paper mills built during the company's first 100 years of operation. The Snoqualmie Falls Lumber Company mill was the first mill built by Weyerhaeuser from the ground up.

161

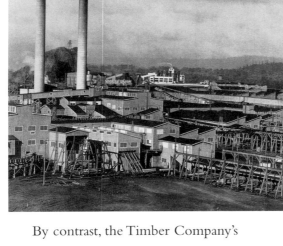

The original sawmills at Longview, Washington, were completed in 1929. They were demolished in 1977, and the NORPAC newsprint mill was constructed on the site.

Opposite: The daily lumber production from the three original Longview mills was approximately 1.2 million board feet. Lumber was either shipped by rail or stored in Longview's mammoth cargo dock, where it was held for maritime transport to worldwide markets.

In 1924, George S. Long stood on a skid road at the company's Camp No. 1, which was located in King County, Washington.

By contrast, the Timber Company's founders set out to ensure continuity through future generations. "What makes us different is that through our history, as now, we have always been oriented toward long-term continuity and growth," George Weyerhaeuser told shareholders in the company's 1988 annual report. Growth was financed through profits for more than half of the 20th century, and the company took on debt conservatively thereafter.

Most of the company's investments in early decades were in timberland, but General Manager George S. Long applied the same spirit of long-term investment to early manufacturing operations. When he recommended the purchase of an Everett, Washington, sawmill in 1902, he had his eye on the future. The mill was small and old, but it had two attractions. One was the site's deepwater harbor, which Long said "undoubtedly would give us all the 'elbow-room' we need for an export mill."[1] The other was the opportunity to dive into manufacturing and learn about Douglas fir.

The mill was purchased and then remodeled on a limited budget to improve efficiency and increase capacity. Long wrote to Frederick Weyerhaeuser that "it looks as though we will have a pretty good mill when we get done; it also looks as though we will spend more money than we originally contemplated."[2]

The experience at Everett convinced the directors that cutting corners with used or second-rate equipment did not pay off. "(T)heir advice to me has always been . . . don't get an old plant, but build a new one that suits you," Long told a colleague as he planned the company's mill at Snoqualmie Falls, Washington.[3] As construction began in 1914, Long noted, "We are putting up a magnificent mill, and I suppose we will be criticized for spending too much money and making everything too good, but the more we reflected on it and the more we thought it over, we felt that that which we are doing was right."[4]

Planning for the future also seemed to guide the purchase of the Longview, Washington, mill site in 1925. Many parcels were for sale along the Columbia River, and the Timber Company took options on several while it decided which to buy.

When the reports came in, instead of choosing one parcel, Long bought several, making Longview the largest mill site in the world. He called the price of more than $234,000 "an enormous investment" for a site, but explained that it would provide flexibility for the future. The site provided access to deep water for shipping and enough space to hold unimagined machinery and unplanned mills that could manufacture the company's nearby timber into whatever forest products that future markets might need.

A QUESTION OF DIVIDENDS

The company's practice of investing in the future included Long's reluctance to pay large dividends whenever he could justify retaining profits for reinvestment.[5] For more than two decades, company founders supported a policy of accumulating attractive timber properties and building capacity for the future, seldom objecting when dividends were small.

In 1926 some shareholders, including William Carson and Dr. E. P. Clapp, supported a buyout by the New York investment bank Goldman Sachs. The proposal met with resistance. Two of Frederick's sons, President John P. Weyerhaeuser and Frederick (F. E.) Weyerhaeuser, considered the mere suggestion unthinkable. Like his father, John believed "the property ought to be kept together and afford an outlet for the future activities of the coming generations, etc."[6]

Although the buyout proposal was never seriously considered, several directors continued to press for more income from their investment. One was F. S. Bell, who was company president from 1928 to 1934. He championed frequent, substantial dividends, but the Great Depression intervened. Weyerhaeuser Timber Company weathered it relatively well, albeit in the red, first in 1930, and again in 1931 and 1932, two years when no dividends were paid.

In 1933, Phil Weyerhaeuser took over as executive vice president, and F. E. Weyerhaeuser, his uncle, replaced Bell as president in 1934. The new leaders championed long-term investment. Earlier in his career, Phil Weyerhaeuser had been general manager of the Clearwater Timber Company, one of several Weyerhaeuser family interests in Idaho. There he had supervised development of a large, modern sawmill outfitted with extras such as water coolers for employees and a cyclone fence around the site for security.[7] Lumbermen running bare-bones operations raised their eyebrows at such amenities.

164

Weyerhaeuser family members and shareholders (from left) Dr. J. R. Jewett, C. A. Weyerhaeuser, Dr. William Hill, F. E. Weyerhaeuser, Snoqualmie Falls Mill Manager W. W. Warren, J. P. Weyerhaeuser, and R. M. Weyerhaeuser inspected the Snoqualmie Falls mill. By 1920, the mill was producing more than 95 million board feet of lumber annually.

The industry became increasingly capital-intensive as harvests took place farther from waterways, technology changed, and wood products became more diverse. Weyerhaeuser Timber Company's earnings grew fast enough to keep up, with the bulk plowed back into new equipment and new businesses. Between 1930 and 1960, these investments, along with the purchase of additional timberlands and facilities, helped the company grow from a handful of operations in two states to a nationwide firm with 80 manufacturing facilities and sales of nearly half a billion dollars.

ONE HUNDRED YEARS OF SHARE VALUE

Meanwhile, the company's forestland increased in value, as did its stock. Assets in 1900 were split among 60,000 shares in the hands of 16 owners who paid $100 per share. The owners increased the company's capital stock each year between 1900 and 1903, expanding the number of shares to 125,000.

Three decades after its incorporation, the Timber Company still had fewer than 300 shareholders, mostly descendants of the original founders. Their investments generally yielded annual dividends of a dollar or two per share. On the rare occasion that a shareholder wanted to sell any shares, the share value was difficult to determine. In the company's first 25 years,

After World War II, Weyerhaeuser Executive Vice President Howard W. Morgan led a companywide effort to improve log utilization. He recommended the manufacture of containerboard at the Springfield, Oregon, complex, using low-grade logs and mill trimmings. Shown is the containerboard's "blow tank bottom" in 1950.

its stock sold for between $200 and $375 per share, with the figure advancing to $850 per share in 1929 as the company's value grew.

The stock split six-for-one in 1931, followed by a four-for-one split in 1937, which increased the shares outstanding to 3 million. As the founders' descendants multiplied, those shares were dispersed and sold to outsiders and by 1950, more than 3,000 people owned Weyerhaeuser Timber Company stock. During the 1940s and 1950s, the company generally returned less than half of its earnings to shareholders as dividends, a ratio lower than that of most other companies.

The company's total return on its large investments in timber and operations rarely exceeded 5 or 6 percent annually,[8] and the dividend policy usually gave shareholders

The 1939 annual report described a seven-year rise in wages, from $.40 an hour to more than $.77 per hour, about 11 percent higher than the industry's average.

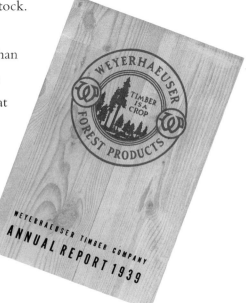

166

Shown celebrating the first day of Weyerhaeuser Company stock trading on the New York Stock Exchange in December 1963 are, from left, Chairman of the Board Frederick K. Weyerhaeuser, Vice President and Director John M. Musser, and investment banker G. Keith Funston.

single-digit return rates on their invested capital, but the company's asset value kept rising, and stock values followed. The rising share values periodically prompted other stock splits, and by 1955, there were 25 million shares outstanding.

Although Weyerhaeuser shares were traded in the over-the-counter market from time to time, they weren't easy to buy or sell, as a current price was not always available. Before the middle of the century, most stock purchasers were already shareholders or their family members.[9] Company managers did relatively little to cooperate with brokers who requested information about earnings, stock prices, or dividends. Annual reports were closely guarded. This lack of public information, which at the time was not required for a closely held company, didn't stop newspapers and firms such as Moody's Investors Service from assembling financial data as best they

could. Consequently, inaccurate Weyerhaeuser Timber Company profit and dividend figures proliferated. During the 1940s, at the urging of the treasurer A. D. Orr, company leaders began distributing annual reports more widely to ensure accurate information.

From 1930 through the 1950s, the numbers of Weyerhaeuser shares and shareholders continued to increase through stock splits and acquisitions. In 1957 the acquisition of Kieckhefer Container Company and Eddy Paper Corporation added over 5 million shares, with other acquisitions adding nearly half a million more.

By 1959, Weyerhaeuser Timber Company had gained the attention of professional investors, who helped increase the ranks of shareholders to more than 10,000.[10] F. E. Weyerhaeuser, president between 1934 and 1945, once told his nephew Phil Weyerhaeuser that interest by "the Wall Street group" would be "very unfortunate."[11] Later, Phil Weyerhaeuser and Laird Bell, chairman of the board beginning in 1947, thought otherwise. They wanted to provide shareholders a more liquid investment.

Under F. K. Weyerhaeuser's chairmanship the board decided to list the stock on the New York Stock Exchange, and in December 1963, the "WY" ticker symbol appeared on both the New York and Pacific Stock Exchanges. By the end of the year, the company had 23,500 stockholders, who earned dividends of $1.20 per share that year.

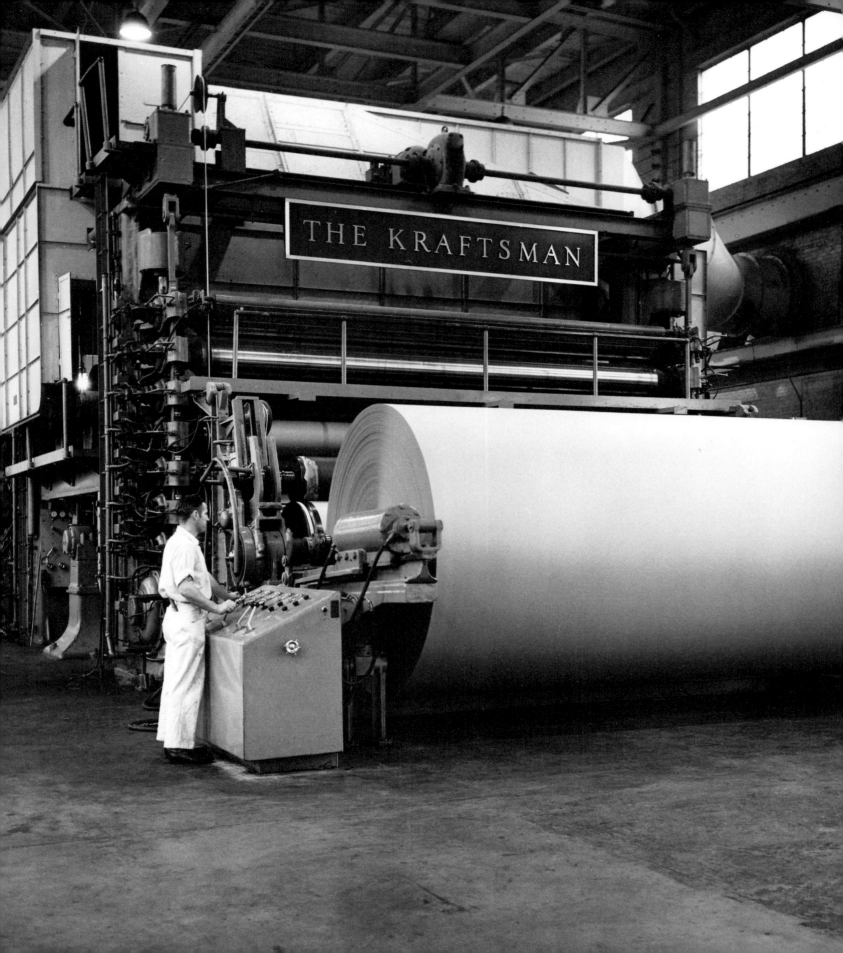

Norton Clapp, like his father, E. P. Clapp, before him, generally favored high dividends. During the late 1950s and the 1960s, dividends represented well over half of the company's earnings, and in some years, as much as 75 percent.

The company's New York Stock Exchange listing in 1963 accelerated a gradual shift toward ownership by institutions and managed funds. By the end of the 20th century, the majority of Weyerhaeuser stock was held by institutional shareholders with different investment interests. While long-term objectives had once outweighed current returns, the company began shifting its focus to achieve both.

SPENDING MONEY TO MAKE MONEY

After more than a half century of financing expansion from profits, Weyerhaeuser assumed long-term debt for the first time in 1964, borrowing $13 million to finance the Kamloops, British Columbia, pulp mill joint venture. Two years later, the company issued $150 million in debenture notes to fund additional business expansions.[12] George Weyerhaeuser, who became president in 1966, said the debt did not mark a change in the company's conservative fiscal strategies but was a natural outcome of healthy growth, secure annual earnings, and the potential for even more growth. Borrowed money helped finance capital investments that included acquisition of forestland and mills in the southern United

States, mill construction and modernization across North America, and another major farsighted investment, High Yield Forestry.

High Yield Forestry called for continuous commitment of capital and management into forestry research, seedling nurseries, site preparation, planting, thinning, and fertilization. "The investments have been huge and have continued through many financial cycles," observed George W. Brown, dean of the College of Forestry at Oregon State University. "I know of no other corporation that has made such a long-term investment."[13] The success of this investment in growing more wood reinforced Weyerhaeuser's faith in the value of building an ever-larger and more productive forest base. Spending patient money to make money continued to be part of the corporate culture.

Employees who joined the company through acquisitions often had to adjust to this philosophy. "Dierks was very cost-conscious," recalled Gil Wooten, who joined Weyerhaeuser along with 3,000 other Dierks Forests employees in a 1969 acquisition. "We had to turn in the old pencil stub to get a new one." Weyerhaeuser spending, by comparison, was

Opposite: Kamloops Pulp and Paper Company's British Columbia timberland under license amounted to 3.8 million acres in 1998. Total company Canadian harvesting rights in 1999 was 33.5 million acres, including forest-lands in Alberta, British Columbia, New Brunswick, Ontario, and Saskatchewan.

169

These Douglas fir logs are of comparable age. The larger log was grown using High Yield Forestry adopted by Weyerhaeuser in 1967, which included planting select seedlings, controlling under-brush, fertilizer applications, and thinning.

Previous pages: The North Fork of the Snoqualmie River runs through the 117,407-acre Snoqualmie Tree Farm, which was established in 1942 on some of the original 45,000 acres that supplied logs to the Snoqualmie Falls Lumber Company mill.

Late in the 1960s the company announced its plan to build a new corporate headquarters 10 miles north of Tacoma, in Federal Way, Washington. The 354,000-square-foot building was designed by the internationally known architectural firm of Skidmore, Owings & Merrill and opened in 1971. The original headquarters building was in Tacoma.

liberal—but so was its income. The company's sales surpassed $1 billion and its profits exceeded $100 million for the first time in 1968. In 1969, after reporting even higher sales and earnings, the annual report announced, "Our intention is to double earnings by 1975."

That goal was achieved early when in 1973 sales hit $2 billion and earnings reached nearly $350 million. Company stock split to 125 million shares held by roughly 30,000 share-holders. Weyerhaeuser's success gained it a favorable reputation among investors, and the company's shares sold at much higher price-to-earnings ratios than competitors' stock. Sales topped $3 billion in 1977, and two years later the company achieved $4 billion in sales and earnings of $512 million.

EXPANSION AND MODERNIZATION

In 1964 only about one-quarter of the company's lands, virtually all in the Northwest, included old-growth forest. Late in 1969, Weyerhaeuser began what would become a $3 billion expansion program, aiming to increase

efficiency, replace aging plants, and begin the transition to high-speed mills that would cut primarily second-growth trees and the typically moderate-size logs grown in Canada's northern climate.

A great deal of new production capacity also was built to use the second- or third-generation trees from or near Weyerhaeuser's southern forestlands. Facilities in Arkansas at Dierks and Mountain Pine, and in Oklahoma at Wright City, acquired from Dierks Forests, were expanded and upgraded. The company also built new sawmills and panel plants in the early 1970s in Mississippi, Alabama, and North Carolina.

At the same time, the company bought and renovated sawmills in British Columbia, Canada, most of which dated back to the 1950s. Weyerhaeuser Canada built a new mill at Vavenby in 1972 to replace three old ones in the vicinity. The new mill included Chip-N-Saw® technology, which could simultaneously make chips and cut lumber from logs under 16 inches in diameter.

In 1976, more versatile equipment and an entirely new sawmill design replaced Longview Mill No. 1, the company's flagship sawmill for more than 40 years. The location of No. 1 became the site of the company's first newsprint plant, NORPAC, which started up in 1979.[14]

Although designed for a variety of log sizes, Longview's new Mill B still accommodated the giants. The eruption of Mount St. Helens in 1980, however, destroyed much of the company's remaining old growth in

the region. The following year, Weyerhaeuser opened its first high-tech mill for small logs at Raymond, Washington. The mill used laser and computer technology to make lumber from logs with average diameters of less than 12 inches.

The company's product mix was changing, too. "Younger trees don't produce the same spectrum of products that older trees do," George Weyerhaeuser explained in 1986. "We are going to have to package smaller and smaller pieces more effectively or remanufacture them into different sizes." Consequently, many Weyerhaeuser facilities built in the 1980s and 1990s, including mills at Grayling, Michigan, and at Moncure and Elkin, North Carolina, made engineered wood and panel products such as oriented strand board.

The company's pulp and paper operations underwent their own evolution. The Longview and Everett pulp and paper operations were upgraded and added product lines. The company invested in linerboard and pulp mills

at Springfield, Oregon, and Cosmopolis, Washington, followed by the 1957 Kieckhefer/Eddy acquisition, which included a pulp and paperboard mill at Plymouth, North Carolina. The 1964 investment in Kamloops Pulp and Paper initiated both the pulp mill and the eventual organization of Weyerhaeuser Canada. In 1969, the company started up a second North Carolina pulp mill, at New Bern, and in 1971, the newly constructed containerboard mill at Valliant, Oklahoma, began operating. Two years later Weyerhaeuser acquired another paper operation, at Rothschild, Wisconsin. Operations at the Plymouth plant were expanded, with the largest fine-paper machine in the world at the time completed in 1975.

The good economic times of the 1970s, along with judicious debt management, also enabled Weyerhaeuser's real estate businesses to grow. The Shelter Group began in 1969 with the acquisitions of the Quadrant Corporation in the Pacific Northwest and Pardee Construction Company in Southern California and Nevada. By 1977, Weyerhaeuser's real-estate operations contributed $47 million in operating earnings.

NAVIGATING THE DOWN CYCLES

The company's financial success of the 1970s did have one negative effect: strict cost control almost became a thing of the past. "We and our American competitors in the 1970s were living in an inflationary environment that put us in

The variety of products made in high-tech small-log mills was different than what could be cut from large logs. Weyerhaeuser opened its first high-tech small-log mill in 1981, in Raymond, Washington.

mode of building rapid growth through capital commitments," reflected George Weyerhaeuser in 1987. "What happens? You forget a lot of the fundamentals."

At the 1980 shareholders' meeting, George warned that falling prices could be expected to squeeze profits. Optimistic, however, he predicted that foresight and discipline would help the company "move successfully through the uncharted waters that lie ahead." He said later in the decade that "I never imagined how many rocks would be in those waters."

With mortgage interest rates approaching 20 percent, the housing industry suffered its worst slump in 50 years. Prices fell across the forest products industry. A strong dollar discouraged purchases by international customers. In 1982 the company's earnings were the lowest in more than a decade. Earnings continued to suffer into the mid-1980s.

Weyerhaeuser in 1982 began a major reorganization aimed to cut costs. The company did away with its regional structure and reduced the number of employees from 48,000 to less than 39,000 by 1985. It curtailed production at unprofitable western lumber operations, sold businesses such as its sack kraft operations that didn't fit the company's primary emphasis, and closed its western Douglas fir plywood plants and other mills that were not competitive.

"We've all got to understand we haven't got a permanent license to capital," George Weyerhaeuser said in 1986. "Your shareholders

will leave you. We have an obligation to them that we are going to meet, which is to say we are going to get earnings up."[15] Weyerhaeuser's consolidated sales were over $6 billion in 1984, but not until 1987 did earnings improve substantially, rising to over $400 million for the first time in the decade.

A major cause of the improvement was overseas sales. Weyerhaeuser had been selling to Japan and Korea since the 1960s. After 12 years of building relationships, the company opened its first office in China in 1984. Weyerhaeuser's total export sales that year exceeded $1.1 billion. In 1986 Weyerhaeuser became the first U.S. forest products company listed on the Tokyo Stock Exchange.[16] A weakening dollar helped boost overseas sales of newsprint, pulp, containerboard, logs, chips, and lumber to $1.5 billion in 1987. In 1988, additional market recovery gave Weyerhaeuser a record $10 billion in sales and record earnings of $564 million, though earnings slid again as the decade turned.

Attending a senior management meeting in the Federal Way headquarters building in 1972 were, from left, Senior Vice President of Corporate Growth C. Calvert Knudsen, Vice President of Fiber Products Businesses Merrill D. Robison, President George H. Weyerhaeuser, Senior Vice President of Wood Products Harry E. Morgan Jr., and Senior Vice President of Administration F. Lowry Wyatt.

Opposite: In the 1990s, Weyerhaeuser produced fine white paper for commercial printing and office use at mills located in Longview, Washington; Rothschild, Wisconsin; Plymouth, North Carolina; Dryden, Ontario; and at the Prince Albert mill in Saskatchewan. Shown is the Columbus mill's coated ground-wood paper machine in 1991.

In the late 1980s, despite higher prices and improved profits, senior management began looking harder at other measures of financial performance, including return on net assets (RONA). At the time, Weyerhaeuser's RONA lagged behind that of its industry competitors. Change was in order. In April 1989, the company began a refocusing effort, and its stock rose more than three points on the day that effort was announced.

The company refocused on the core businesses it could most profitably grow. A number of operations, including the company's salmon ranching, hydroponic food products, and garden-supply businesses, were shut down or sold over the next few years. According to the 1990 annual report, the operations that were eliminated "once accounted for nearly $1 billion of our sales but, taken together, virtually none of our profits." More businesses, including Shemin Nurseries, were earmarked for sale later in the decade when market conditions were more favorable. Some, such as Republic Savings and Loan, were eventually shut down when no buyer materialized. The company took special charges for severance pay, write-offs, and other restructuring costs in 1989 and 1991. These charges amounted to over a half billion dollars, with the 1991 charge creating a net loss.

Analysts regarded the Weyerhaeuser that emerged from the refocusing effort as "a stronger, more streamlined company."[17] Employees renewed emphasis on improving productivity, increasing the reliability of manufacturing processes, controlling costs, and serving customers.

The improvements allowed the company to increase shareholder dividends and also to repurchase 11 million shares of stock, leaving approximately 200 million shares outstanding. While that number of shares outstanding was much larger than earlier in the century, most of the increase had come through splits of existing stock. Weyerhaeuser's bond ratings and its relatively low debt-to-capital ratio, usually between 35 and 45 percent, had not changed much since the company first took on long-term debt in the 1960s. "A lot of our assets are very long-term assets," said Bill Stivers, executive vice president and chief financial officer, "and you don't put them at risk with a highly leveraged capital structure."

Stivers said, however, that a "prudent" amount of debt allowed the company to keep growing and to make investments that would enhance the return to shareholders. The company invested in its core businesses with the 1992 acquisition of two Procter & Gamble pulp mills in Alberta, Canada, and Georgia, along with sawmills and forestlands; two major forestland acquisitions; a joint venture to build an Iowa containerboard mill that opened in 1996 using exclusively recycled fiber; and a 1998 purchase from Bowater that gained the company a paper mill, two lumber mills, and associated timber licenses in Ontario.

Weyerhaeuser successfully strengthened its financial performance through 1995, with the last half of the decade bringing deteriorating company and industry economic conditions and resulting declines in margins.

BUILDING ON SUCCESS

When Steve Rogel became Weyerhaeuser president in 1997, he said, "My job now is to build upon this foundation of success." He established a RONA target of 17 percent (at the company level), explaining, "That happens to be about where the very best company in this industry operates." A strong emphasis on manufacturing efficiency and cost control will consistently produce strong financial performance, when coupled with a judicious use of capital.

During the 1990s capital expenditures reached a billion dollars each year to keep up with facility modernizations, process innovations, computer technology, and environmental regulations. Methods for considering major investments needed more discipline. Under Rogel, the company aggressively moved ahead with processes to ensure that investments helped achieve financial goals.

As part of its more disciplined approach to capital, Weyerhaeuser employed two strategies: buying rather than building, and using partnerships such as the World Timberfund to pool resources for investments. Both strategies positioned the company to play a key role in the consolidation that was likely to mark the industry's future.

Perhaps the greatest example of the buy strategy occurred as the 20th century came to a close. In an interview shortly after he joined the company as president, Steve Rogel envisioned a future where Weyerhaeuser's growth would occur through acquisition and consolidation rather than building new capacity. He cited several examples in which companies with similar asset bases, values, and corporate cultures were able to combine to create even greater companies and stated that Weyerhaeuser would be looking for similar opportunities. "The value of such industry consolidation lies not in growth for its own sake but in bringing

Retired President and Chief Executive Officer John W. "Jack" Creighton Jr. (on left) and the company's then newly elected President and Chief Executive Officer, Steven R. Rogel, in April 1998.

Left: Loaded and ready for transportation to mid-North American markets, this oriented strand board (OSB) was produced at the Drayton Valley mill in Alberta, Canada.

177

two companies with complementary strengths together into a single organization more successful than either could be individually," said Rogel.

Rogel's vision was realized less than two years later, when Weyerhaeuser acquired MacMillan Bloedel, a Canada-based company with 1998 sales of $2.9 billion (US). In June 1999, when the offer was made, MacMillan Bloedel was one of Canada's largest forest products firms. It consisted of three container-board mills, 19 packaging plants, three oriented strand board (OSB) mills, nine lumber or plywood mills, and 31 building materials distribution centers. It also held shares in several joint ventures and had 6.9 million acres of forestland in ownership and harvesting rights from British Columbia to Alabama.

"MacMillan Bloedel represents an excellent strategic fit with us in terms of assets, values, and culture," said Rogel.

The two companies' histories were similar, too. The Canadian company's roots reached nearly as far back in the 20th century as Weyerhaeuser's. MacMillan Bloedel began in 1901 as Brooks–Scanlon, a Minnesota-based forest products company that invested heavily in British Columbia forestlands. In 1909, the firm became known as Powell River Paper Company, Ltd., and entered the newsprint industry, later becoming a large producer of market pulp.

About the same time, Wisconsin native Julius Harold Bloedel and a number of partners began investing in railroads, mining operations, lumber mills, and Pacific Northwest forestland, including timber stands around Powell River. Growth in British Columbia also caught the attention of Ontario native Harvey Reginald MacMillan, who founded H. R. MacMillan Export Company in 1919 and would come to be known as "the greatest entrepreneur in B.C. history."[18] The first to ship West Coast lumber through the newly opened Panama Canal, MacMillan later expanded to managing forestland and manufacturing lumber, plywood, railroad ties, and doors.

Bloedel attempted to acquire MacMillan's interests in 1950 and was rebuffed, but a year later the companies came together as MacMillan & Bloedel Limited. In 1960, the company merged with Powell River and began an impressive period of globalization. Before the end of the decade, MacMillan Bloedel built containerboard plants in Europe, Asia, and

H. R. MacMillan founded his first company, a lumber export enterprise, in 1919. In 1951, he joined with the Bloedel family and formed MacMillan & Bloedel Limited. Shown in 1903 is H. R. MacMillan (second from right) as a student at Ontario Agricultural College.

Opposite: Since their development in 1959, 10,000-horse-power "Mars" water bombers have been used to fight fires in remote British Columbia forestland. In a six-hour shift, each of the two World War II flying boats (converted into water bombers by former MacMillan Bloedel senior executive pilot Dan McIvor), could load and drop a 60,000-pound payload 30 times. Each drop drenched up to three acres in a dense cloud of fire retardant.

179

GTH 237 FT.
ETER AT BUTT 4 FT. TOP 14 INCHES.
S SCANLON, O'BRIEN CO.
LLWATER B.C. June 22nd 1912

180

Shown are members of a Brooks, Scanlon & O'Brien Company crew with a 237-foot Douglas fir flagpole cut on Vancouver Island, British Columbia, for shipment to London, England. Brooks-Scanlon began acquiring Vancouver Island forestland in the early 1900s. These holdings were merged with those of John O'Brien in 1908, and their company became part of MacMillan Bloedel when it merged with Powell River Paper Company in 1960. Photo courtesy of Special Collections and University Archives Division, University of British Columbia.

the United States, and invested millions to build the Canadian Transport Company. In 1966 the company became known as MacMillan Bloedel and was Canada's largest exporter of finished lumber.[19]

In 1976, following a profit-sapping industrywide recession, MacMillan Bloedel hired C. Calvert Knudsen, a senior vice president at Weyerhaeuser, as its new president. During his tenure, MacMillan Bloedel adopted a number of Weyerhaeuser systems for planning and capital investment.[20] Perhaps it wasn't surprising that the two companies steered through similar diversification strategies during the late 1970s and 1980s. Weyerhaeuser began refocusing on its core businesses in the late 1980s, and

MacMillan Bloedel engaged in a similar process when it appointed Tom Stephens as its new president and chief executive officer in 1997. He resolved long-standing environmental and safety issues, in addition to bringing the company's employees into more active roles in managing its operations. He sold the company's vast pulp and paper business and the Canadian Transport Company. When the company's packaging operations were offered for sale, Weyerhaeuser became interested. "We liked it so much, we wanted to buy the whole company," recalled Steve Rogel.[21]

When it joined Weyerhaeuser in 1999, MacMillan Bloedel had more than 9,500 employees. Weyerhaeuser's executive vice president of Wood Products, Bill Corbin, said, "We have similar values, and we think alike when it comes to safety and profitably serving markets and customers."

As the two companies united, Weyerhaeuser publicly committed itself to implementing MacMillan Bloedel's variable retention harvesting practices in coastal British Columbia. This innovative approach to forest harvests increased protection of old-growth timber and improved habitat variety. Weyerhaeuser also promised to honor MacMillan Bloedel's commitments to communities, First Nations, and environmental interests, including the Clayoquot Accord, regarding the development of new approaches to coastal old-growth forests with high conservation values. Rogel observed, "We can learn lessons from MacMillan Bloedel's restructuring, from its innovative forestry in the coastal areas of British Columbia, from its partnerships with aboriginals, and from its bold performance targets."

The acquisition demonstrated Weyerhaeuser's consolidation at its best. It precluded the need for building new capacity, while ensuring that customer demand was met and showing the cost advantages of acquiring existing capacity. Additionally, the single combined organization with a new structure further supported Weyerhaeuser's strategy for a unified North American company. The public name for Weyerhaeuser's operations in Canada became simply "Weyerhaeuser." Bill Gaynor, the president of what was formerly known as Weyerhaeuser Canada, Ltd., joined the company's Senior Management Team, a Canadian director from MacMillan Bloedel's board of directors joined Weyerhaeuser's board, and business units in Canada reported through the North American business leaders. "This emphasizes our commitment to operate as a single North American company and present a single face to all of our stakeholders," said Rogel. "Beginning our second century as one consolidated company further strengthens our position as a competitor on a global scale and as the finest forest products company in the world."

Benchman Bruno Canil is shown in 1997 preparing a cut-off saw blade for use in MacMillan Bloedel's Powell River mill. Like Weyerhaeuser, MacMillan Bloedel used thin-blade technology to maximize the amount of high-value lumber cut from each log.

181

Opposite: Forester Brad Kuegel marked selected trees for thinning from a 20-year-old stand of southern pine that was grown using High Yield Forestry principles on Weyerhaeuser forestland near New Bern, North Carolina.

A small part of Weyerhaeuser's "woodpile," the log yard at its Green Mountain, Washington, mill, is near the 473,000-acre St. Helens Tree Farm.

ACHIEVING A BALANCE

Asset productivity is a significant issue for a company with $17 billion in assets. "Somebody once said to me, 'It's easy to be complacent when you're sitting on the world's biggest woodpile,'" George Weyerhaeuser recalled. "That's easy to say, but we haven't been complacent. We've been adding to the company's value. We've been growing and improving the trees. We've been growing the technology." He continued, "The land base and tree crops now have a greater potential than ever."

Weyerhaeuser would begin to realize that potential over the first decade of the 21st century, as thousands of acres of its High Yield Forests reached harvest age. To capitalize on this bounty as the 20th century came to a close, Weyerhaeuser businesses were building new customer relationships and exploring new markets for the future.

The concept of long-term planning for the future was ingrained in Weyerhaeuser leaders. The company's history demonstrated the value of taking the long view. An emphasis on continuity was also reflected in the company's money management. "We've had very consistent financial strategies over a very long time," Stivers said. He pointed to policies documented in 1973 that focus on maintaining a sound, conservative capital structure, protecting shareholders' interests, having consistent access to capital, and managing debt to minimize risk.

People sometimes called Weyerhaeuser "risk averse"; nothing could be more off the mark. From the initial forest purchase through sustainable forestry, tree farming, High Yield Forestry, and expansion into international markets, Weyerhaeuser has undertaken pioneering leadership at significant, calculated risk, and with great success.

Nothing ventured—nothing gained, and the company's new ventures weren't always as successful as planned. "The company still strives to be the best," said George Weyerhaeuser Jr. "We have a fuller understanding that being the best means providing investors a healthy return today, as well as planning for tomorrow."

Achieving that balance was one of Steve Rogel's objectives. "What I have to do," he said, "is show people that we can earn more, give more to the shareholder, and still have some extra left to reinvest in our business. I firmly believe we can do that."

CHAPTER SIX

Foundation for the Future

"When you talk with employees about Weyerhaeuser, they want the company to be number one," said Mike Bickford, who is responsible for the company's corporate advertising. "They want to win the championship." Dave Elkin, Weyerhaeuser's Arkansas/Oklahoma Timberlands manager, echoed this remark: "There isn't anybody here who doesn't want to be the best."

As Weyerhaeuser entered the 21st century, its challenge was to be "the best forest products company in the world," and the company's value system was the cornerstone of this achievement. "What we bring to the table is a set of core values we all truly believe in," said Dick Gozon, executive vice president of Pulp, Paper and Packaging. "Embedded in the company we work for are things that really matter." They ensure the company's continuity.

Those corporate values—respect for all people, integrity, partnerships with customers, environmental stewardship, and financial commitments to shareholders—shaped the company's history. "The purpose of looking back," said retired Chairman of the Board George Weyerhaeuser, "is to develop some sense of direction and continuity while conditions around us are changing."

A VALUE SYSTEM THAT GROWS

As president, chairman, and chief executive officer, Steve Rogel will lead the company into the 21st century. When George Weyerhaeuser retired as Weyerhaeuser's chairman of the board in 1999 after completing 50 years of service, including 25 as chief executive, he said he'd like his own final accomplishments to

Opposite: Weyerhaeuser has planted 50 million to 200 million seedlings annually as part of its commitment to High Yield Forestry. Shown is the company's Washington, North Carolina, pine nursery.

185

On a tour of the company's Olympia, Washington, box plant in 1998, CEO Steve Rogel (center) asked general managers and machine tenders alike about Weyerhaeuser production processes. Shown with Rogel are knife operator Mitch McManus (left) and assistant knife operator Fred Gustafson (right).

Opposite: McKenzie Reed inspected fine paper being produced at the Plymouth, North Carolina, mill.

Right: Shown is a plantation-grown pine log being processed at the Dierks, Arkansas, mill.

Following pages: Weyerhaeuser's corporate headquarters building is set in a 500-acre site, among Douglas fir, lakes, and lupine.

186

include handing on the corporate principles inherited by his generation of Weyerhaeuser employees. "The guiding principles are fundamentals that carry on through," he said. "They are evident in the company's response to change, and the shifting expectations of customers, shareholders, and the public. In turn, the events of the past refined the values that continue to make Weyerhaeuser successful."

Steve Hill, senior vice president of human resources, recalled an instance during the 1980s when he became uncomfortable with a proposed change to an employee benefit plan. "I went to see George Weyerhaeuser, and I'll never forget how much he listened and asked good questions," Hill said. "He made a decision that was not consistent with what I wanted to do. But he also called me and explained to me why he had made the decision and acknowledged that I had done absolutely the right thing to raise my concern. My experience here has always been that if you really felt that the level of integrity was inconsistent with the

value system, there were people you could talk to." For employees who are uncomfortable or unable to discuss concerns directly with senior managers, Weyerhaeuser's Business Conduct Committee offered a confidential alternative.

Weyerhaeuser's values both guide company conduct and define its relationships with employees, customers, shareholders, and the public. In the early 1990s, when senior managers laid out the vision of Weyerhaeuser being "the best forest products company in the world," employees asked for clarification. Weyerhaeuser already was the largest marketer of softwood lumber in the world, the largest producer of market pulp, and owner of the largest private volume of softwood timber forest in the world. Employees wanted to know what criteria defined *best*. Creighton advised, "We'll know we're the best when our major stakeholders—our employees, our customers, our shareholders, and the communities where we do business—tell us we are."[1]

Weyerhaeuser already enjoyed considerable recognition from those stakeholders. Customers, for instance, credited Weyerhaeuser with being the best supplier in a variety of market segments, including some—such as fine paper—where the company can't claim sheer size. "I'm prejudiced, but for good reasons," explained David McGehee, executive vice president of Mac Papers, a paper distributor in the southeastern United States. "There have been numerous independent surveys, and Weyerhaeuser consistently is on top."

Bruce Zobel, an international forestry consultant who worked with dozens of forest products companies worldwide, said, "Weyerhaeuser is clearly the best, most innovative, and progressive of the group. Everywhere I work, Weyerhaeuser is looked upon as the world leader in forestry."[2]

Rather than rest on such recognition as the company celebrated its centennial, Rogel and other employees focused on the pivotal challenges to the future objectives. For example,

As part of Weyerhaeuser's strategy to expand its uncoated free sheet paper business, the company acquired the Dryden, Ontario, fine paper mill (and several sawmills) from Bowater in 1998. The banner in the photo below proclaimed the Dryden mill's enviable safety record.

the company had been known for its slow and measured style of decision making. "We really want to have the facts and a thorough understanding before we make a decision," noted biologist Tony Melchiors. "It's a real strength." On the other hand, said Gozon, "When you get everybody involved in the decision-making process, it's painfully slow. We just really, really have to pick up the pace."

"The things I would like to see instilled here are speed, simplicity, decisiveness," Rogel said. Still a newcomer at the time, he acknowledged Weyerhaeuser employees' deep-seated desire to change and to become the best: "That commitment is all over the place," he said. More stringent decision-making processes for capital investment and the coordination of purchasing across the company had been applied in the mid-1990s. Rogel not only carried forth these initiatives but also applied similar approaches to increasing efficiency and eliminating redundancies among other companywide activities such as information technology, support services, and research and development.

The board of directors had such a transition in mind when they selected Rogel as the company's 11th president, noted George Weyerhaeuser. "There's a time and a place for more vision," he said, "and there's a time and a place to run it tighter and run it tougher on the premise that the biggest challenges ahead are the highly competitive conditions. Jack set some objectives, and Steve is leading the execution and delivery, and we're going to be out front, not down in the middle somewhere."

To get out front and remain there, Rogel and senior managers created an integrated set of companywide behaviors, objectives, processes, and goals called the "Roadmap for Success." Built on Weyerhaeuser's strong base of values, the goals included a return on net assets (RONA) of 19 percent (at the business level) averaged across the business cycle. To earn this RONA, the roadmap identified 10 specific processes the company would use to improve its performance, including a more disciplined approach to capital investment, a value-oriented method for deciding which products and services to offer customers, and processes to obtain maximum leverage of the resources

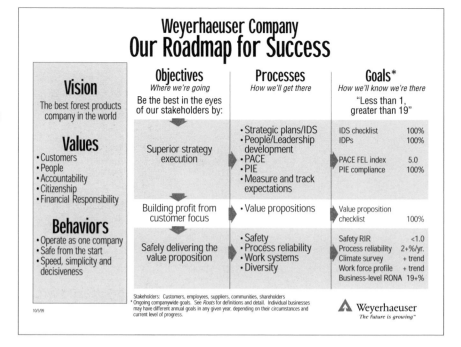

and advantages of being a large company. A specific goal was set for each process. For instance, employees across the company would use similar techniques to increase production efficiency by making the manufacturing processes themselves more reliable and consistent. Through proven practices for work such as preventive maintenance and standard machine setup, they planned to increase process reliability by an average of 2 percent or more each year. That ongoing improvement rate was expected not only to ensure that customers got exactly what they wanted, when they wanted it, but also to reduce waste, minimize manufacturing costs, and prevent environmental incidents such as spills.

"If we follow this roadmap, our financial performance will match its potential," said Rogel. "I expect the roadmap to last us many years."

President Rogel's "Roadmap for Success."

Following pages: Located near Enumclaw, Washington, in the Cascade Range under the shadow of Mount Rainier, the White River Tree Farm was established in 1944.

191

Comprised of owned and leased land, Weyerhaeuser's southern United States forestlands in 1998 totaled more than 3.36 million acres of pine and hardwood species. Collectively, this forestland served as the principal resource base for the company's 30 southern United States mills.

Opposite: Shown is an interior view of the Kamloops pulp and paper complex in 1997.

194

VALUES IN THE 21ST CENTURY

During the new century, as in the past, changes at Weyerhaeuser would be based on the values that have sustained the company during its 100 years: respect for people, integrity, partnerships with customers, stewardship of the environment, and financial responsibility to shareholders. Senior managers were convinced that these values would ensure Weyerhaeuser's continued longevity and success. "Companies without good value systems are the ones that have the most trouble surviving over the long haul," Rogel observed.

Company leaders believed that the people of Weyerhaeuser would achieve its goal of being the best. "Our timber is unmatched. We have great facilities in place. Our research and development capabilities are world-renowned. We have one of the strongest balance sheets in the industry. In short, we have the tools to become the best forest products company in the world," Rogel asserted in the 1998 annual report. "Weyerhaeuser is a great company. It has a promising future. Our challenge is to fulfill our potential."

The company has been fulfilling its potential since 1900, when Frederick Weyerhaeuser and his fellow investors paid more than $5 million for an unknown quantity of a timber species they had never milled. George S. Long saw that potential when he rode a coal-powered train for four days to take on the job of company manager in a state he had never seen. That potential was still in mind when employees stepped up to new computers, acquired timber on the other side of the world, gave up the security of old roles for new ones—or welcomed a new president who was guaranteed to bring change, and one who respected the company's values. The challenge to the company's future, according to President Steve Rogel, is "the wise use of Weyerhaeuser's resources, economic strength, and technical expertise in the pursuit of profitable business.

"I came into a company with a great, proud history," Rogel said. "The fact that we are 100 years old shows that the values have stood the test of time, and in the end, it's the value system that will carry us through."

Footnotes

PREFACE

1. F. K. Weyerhaeuser and John Musser, 1953, oral history transcript in the Weyerhaeuser Archives Collection, p. 44
2. George S. Long letter to A. C. McNeill, August 12, 1920

INTRODUCTION

1. *Timber and Men*, p. 6
2. *Where the Future Grows*, p. 6
3. *Timber and Men*, p. 213
4. W. L. McCormick letter to E. P. Clapp, September 16, 1924

CHAPTER ONE

1. George H. Weyerhaeuser, interview on videotape by Michael Parks, August 14, 1987
2. *Frederick Weyerhaeuser: A Pen Portrait*, p. 7
3. *Timber and Men*, p. 588
4. Ibid., p. 53
5. *George S. Long*, p. 5; *Timber and Men,* p. 216
6. *George S. Long*, p. 325
7. Ibid., p. 34
8. *George S. Long*, p. 54; *Weyerhaeuser Company History, 1974*, p. 12
9. *Historical Statistics of the United States,* p. 163
10. *Logging with Steam in the Pacific Northwest*, p. xiv
11. *From Jamestown to Coffin Rock*, p. 13
12. *George S. Long*, p. 350
13. *From Jamestown to Coffin Rock*, p. 89
14. *George S. Long*, p. 195

15. John P. Weyerhaeuser letter to Hunt Taylor, November 22, 1917, as noted in Kohlmeyer, Fred W., "The Labor Movement: Collective Bargaining," and *Timber and Men* working papers in the Weyerhaeuser Archives Collection, Record Group 7, p. 47
16. *I.W.W. Songbook*, Industrial Workers of the World, 1916, Weyerhaeuser Archives Collection
17. *Phil Weyerhaeuser*, p. 140
18. Kohlmeyer, Fred W., "The Labor Movement: Collective Bargaining," and *Timber and Men* working papers in the Weyerhaeuser Archives Collection, Record Group 7, p. 48; *George S. Long*, p. 210
19. *From Jamestown to Coffin Rock*, p. 220
20. Ibid., p. 174
21. *George S. Long*, p. 105
22. Compilation from government reports prepared by the Lumberman's Industrial Relations Committee, Inc., Series 6, Chart No. 3, December 1938; also found in LIRC Series 6, Facts Washington, No. 1, Weyerhaeuser Archives Collection
23. T. S. Durment oral history transcript in the Weyerhaeuser Archives Collection, p. 27
24. *From Jamestown to Coffin Rock*, p. 209
25. *Men, Mills and Timber*, p. 47
26. Thomas, Norman, "Labor: General," *Timber and Men* working papers in the Weyerhaeuser Archives Collection, Record Group 7, p. 2; *Timber and Men*, p. 570
27. *From Jamestown to Coffin Rock*, p. 79
28. Ibid., p. 248
29. Ibid.
30. *Weyerhaeuser Magazine*, February 1964
31. *Weyerhaeuser World*, May 1970

32. Weyerhaeuser 1971 Annual Report

33. *Tacoma News Tribune*, October 31, 1990; "Rip Van Weyerhaeuser," *Forbes*, October 28, 1991; *Weyerhaeuser Today*, February 1992; *Puget Sound Business Journal*, South Sound/Pierce County Edition, December 3, 1990

34. Weyerhaeuser *Connection* newsletter, September 1996

35. *Weyerhaeuser Today* article, May 1996

36. Weyerhaeuser *Connection* newsletter, January 1998

37. Weyerhaeuser *QualityWorks* newsletter, Third Quarter 1996

38. Weyerhaeuser *Connection* newsletter, August 1997

39. *Weyerhaeuser Today,* December 1996

40. *George S. Long*, p. 303

41. *Weyerhaeuser World*, October 1970

42. T. S. Durment oral history transcript in the Weyerhaeuser Archives Collection, p. 3; *From Jamestown to Coffin Rock*, p. 186

43. *Weyerhaeuser Magazine,* May 1950; *In the Chips*, p. 214

44. *In the Chips*, p. 156

45. *George S. Long*, p. 171

46. *In the Chips*, p. 132

47. *Phil Weyerhaeuser*, p. 271

CHAPTER TWO

1. *Where the Future Grows*, p. 45

2. *Timber and Men*, p. 7

3. Ibid., p. 61

4. *F. K. Weyerhaeuser*, p. 13

5. *George S. Long,* p. 102

6. *George S. Long*, p. 392; *Timber and Men*, p. 236

7. *George S. Long*, p. 25

8. Gardner, Gilson, "Timber Famine in 60 Years if We Keep on Cutting," November 23, 1909, from the Weyerhaeuser Archives Collection; *Phil Weyerhaeuser*, p. 183

9. *Longview* (Washington) *Daily News*, February 25, 1984

10. *George S. Long*, pp. 78, 96

11. *The Lumber World*, Chicago, Illinois, January 1, 1907, p. 6

12. Emerson Hough, "The Slaughter of the Trees," *Everybody's*, as referenced in *Timber and Men*, p. 303

13. *F. K. Weyerhaeuser*, p. 256

14. Ibid., pp. 85-6

15. *Where the Future Grows*, p. 17

16. Weyerhaeuser press release, September 24, 1976

17. *George S. Long*, p. 260; *Timber and Men*, pp. 305-9

18. *Timber and Men*, p. 448

19. *Weyerhaeuser Today*, December 1996

20. *George S. Long*, p. 103

21. Ibid., p. 303

22. Ibid., p. 101

23. Ibid., p. 397

24. *Phil Weyerhaeuser*, p. 174

25. Ibid., p. 185

26. Ibid., pp. 183, 187

27. Ibid., pp. 187, 191

28. Ibid., p. 192

29. *Phil Weyerhaeuser*, p. 238; *From Jamestown to Coffin Rock*, p. 259

30. *Phil Weyerhaeuser*, p. 197

31. *Weyerhaeuser Magazine,* August 1959

32. *Weyerhaeuser Magazine*, August 1957; *Weyerhaeuser World*, January 1970

33. "Awareness of the Weyerhaeuser Name and Magazine Advertising," Opinion Research Corporation, Princeton, New Jersey, 1952, 1956, 1962

34. Freedgood, Seymour, "Weyerhaeuser Timber: Out of the Woods," *Fortune*, September 1959

35. *Weyerhaeuser Magazine*, October 1959

36. *Weyerhaeuser World*, October 1970

37. *Weyerhaeuser Today*, March 1993

38. *Puget Sound Business Journal*, December 23-29, 1994

39. Ibid.

40. Weyerhaeuser 1995 Annual Environmental Performance Report

CHAPTER THREE

1. *George S. Long*, p. 29
2. Ibid., p. 270
3. Ibid., p. 181
4. *F. K. Weyerhaeuser*, p. 67
5. *Where the Future Grows*, p. 14 (photo)
6. *George S. Long*, p. 279; *Timber and Men*, p. 357
7. *Where the Future Grows*, p. 16
8. *George S. Long*, p. 323
9. Ibid., pp. 354-5
10. *Where the Future Grows*, p. 18
11. *From Jamestown to Coffin Rock*, p. 185
12. *Where the Future Grows*, p. 18
13. *George S. Long*, pp. 394-5
14. *F. K. Weyerhaeuser*, p. 124
15. Ibid., pp. 119-20
16. Ibid., p. 257
17. *From Jamestown to Coffin Rock*, p. 192
18. *Where the Future Grows*, p. 21
19. George H. Weyerhaeuser, 1986, oral history transcript in the Weyerhaeuser Archives Collection, p. 27; *In the Chips*, p. 93
20. *In the Chips*, p. 21
21. Ibid., p. 22
22. *Where the Future Grows*, p. 21
23. *In the Chips*, pp. 151-2; *Weyerhaeuser Magazine*, September 1959, p. 8
24. Ibid., p. 8
25. *In the Chips*, p. 296
26. *Timber and Men*, pp. 479-80
27. Ibid., pp. 482-3
28. B. L. Adams letter to C. Ingram, November 17, 1952
29. Bruce Collins airgram to E. A. Miller, May 27, 1952
30. *In the Chips*, p. 136-9
31. *Weyerhaeuser Magazine*, June 1959, p. 11
32. Freedgood, Seymour, "Weyerhaeuser Timber: Out of the Woods," *Fortune*, September 1959

33. *Where the Future Grows*, p. 27
34. *Phil Weyerhaeuser*, pp. 132, 204; *F. K. Weyerhaeuser*, p. 267
35. *Phil Weyerhaeuser*, p. 214
36. *In the Chips*, p. 489
37. Ibid., p. 739
38. *The Roanoke* (North Carolina) *Beacon*, 1982 special supplement on the 25th anniversary of Weyerhaeuser in North Carolina, p. 3
39. Weyerhaeuser 1962 Annual Report
40. George H. Weyerhaeuser, 1986, oral history transcript in the Weyerhaeuser Archives Collection, pp. 118-9
41. *In the Chips*, p. 766
42. *Where the Future Grows*, p. 44
43. George H. Weyerhaeuser as interviewed by Linda Edgerly, 1986, oral history transcript in the Weyerhaeuser Archives Collection, p. 176
44. Weyerhaeuser 1977 Annual Report
45. "The Customer Speaks," Weyerhaeuser *Customer Satisfaction* newsletter, December 1988

CHAPTER FOUR

1. *George S. Long*, p. 30
2. *Timber and Men*, p. 594
3. *George S. Long*, p. 120
4. Ibid., p. 107
5. Ibid., p. 131
6. Ibid., pp. 325-6
7. *From Jamestown to Coffin Rock*, p. 17
8. *Where the Future Grows*, p. 16
9. Transcript of the Senate Select Committee on Reforestation Hearings, 1922

10. *George S. Long*, p. 296;
    Where the Future Grows, p. 16

11. *Where the Future Grows*, p. 16

12. Norman E. Borlaug letter to Rex McCullough,
    October 17, 1994

13. *George S. Long*, p. 373

14. *From Jamestown to Coffin Rock*, p. 84

15. *Phil Weyerhaeuser*, p. 228

16. *Phil Weyerhaeuser*, pp. 125, 157

17. Ibid., pp. 169-70

18. Ibid., p. 212

19. Ibid., p. 231

20. *Timber and Men*, p. 503

21. *Phil Weyerhaeuser*, p. 230

22. Cited in "The Changing Relationship Between
    Forest Industry and the American Public,"
    Dr. Steven Anderson, presented January 31, 1998

23. Cited in *A Celebration for Generations to Come*

24. American Tree Farm System data cited in
    A Celebration for Generations to Come

25. *Timber and Men,* p. 504

26. Ed Heacox oral history transcript in the High
    Yield Forestry collection of the Weyerhaeuser
    Archives Collection, October 30, 1987

27. Interviewer W. Lawrence in Ed Heacox oral
    history transcript in the High Yield Forestry
    collection of the Weyerhaeuser Archives
    Collection, October 30, 1987

28. F. K. Weyerhaeuser speech to the Forest Industry
    Open Symposium, Chicago, April 21, 1966,
    in the Weyerhaeuser Archives Collection

29. Ed Heacox oral history transcript in the High
    Yield Forestry collection of the Weyerhaeuser
    Archives Collection, October 30, 1987

30. Ibid.

31. "Industrial forest research and forest science,"
    Forest Science, Harold R. Steen, editor (in press);
    Where the Future Grows, p. 34

32. *F. K. Weyerhaeuser*, p. 236

33. *In the Chips*, p. 734

34. High Yield Forestry presentation to the Board
    of Directors in the Weyerhaeuser Archives
    Collection, H. E. Morgan Jr., 1968

35. "Best of the S.O.B.s," John Mitchell, *The
    Audubon Society Magazine*, September 1974;
    "Weyerhaeuser Gets Set for the 21st Century,"
    Thomas Griffith, *Fortune*, April 1977

36. *Innovations and Trees*, 1975

37. David B. Thorud letter to Rex McCullough,
    October 20, 1994

38. John C. Gordon letter to Rex McCullough,
    October 6, 1994

39. Weyerhaeuser 1977 Annual Report

40. *Men, Mills and Timber*, p. 22

41. *Phil Weyerhaeuser*, p. 363

42. *Where the Future Grows*, p. 29

43. "Weyerhaeuser Gets Set for the 21st Century,"
    Thomas Griffith, *Fortune*, April 1977;
    Weyerhaeuser 1972 Annual Report

44. "Weyerhaeuser Gets Set for the 21st Century,"
    Thomas Griffith, *Fortune*, April 1977;
    Weyerhaeuser 1973 Annual Report

45. Weyerhaeuser *Environmental Stewardship* brochure
    and other company sources

46. *Where the Future Grows*, p. 34

47. *In the Chips*, p. 138

48. Ibid., pp. 138-42

49. Ibid., p. 590

50. "Best of the S.O.B.'s," John Mitchell,
    The Audubon Society Magazine, September 1974

51. "An Ecologist in the Paper Industry,"
Business Week, March 6, 1971

52. *In the Chips*, p. 764

53. "Best of the S.O.B.s," John Mitchell,
The Audubon Society Magazine, September 1974

54. "What Worries Weyerhaeuser," Dan Sellard,
Eugene (Oregon) *Register-Guard*,
November 12, 1972

55. "Weyerhaeuser Gets Set for the 21st Century,"
Thomas Griffith, *Fortune*, April 1977

56. "Industrial forest research and forest science,"
Forest Science, Harold R. Steen, editor (in press)

57. Weyerhaeuser 1997 annual environmental
performance report

58. "Why Weyerhaeuser's Prospects Look Bright,"
Jay Palmer, *Barron's*, October 25, 1993

59. "The New Growth at Weyerhaeuser,"
Dori Jones Yang, *Business Week*, June 19, 1995

60. *Weyerhaeuser Today*, February 1994

CHAPTER FIVE

1. *George S. Long,* p. 46

2. Ibid., p. 63

3. Ibid., p. 168

4. Ibid., p. 173

5. Ibid., p. 256

6. Ibid., p. 328

7. *Phil Weyerhaeuser,* p. 66

8. *George S. Long,* p. 353; *F. K. Weyerhaeuser,* p. 154

9. *Phil Weyerhaeuser,* p. 40

10. *Timber and Men*, p. 571

11. *Phil Weyerhaeuser,* p. 239

12. *Where the Future Grows*, p. 39

13. George W. Brown letter to Rex McCullough,
September 23, 1994

14. Weyerhaeuser 1976 Annual Report

15. George H. Weyerhaeuser, 1986, oral history
transcript in the Weyerhaeuser Archives
Collection, p. 362

16. *Where the Future Grows*, p. 55

17. "Weyerhaeuser Picks Rogel as New CEO,"
Kara Swisher, *Wall Street Journal*,
November 18, 1997

18. "The Giant Falls South," Jennifer Hunter,
Maclean's, July 5, 1999

19. Ross Hay-Roe, founder of *PaperTree Letter*
(Miller Freeman: San Francisco), interview by
Kevin Gudridge for *Marple's Business Newsletter*,
July 21, 1999

20. *Empire of Wood* pp. 318–9

21. "The Giant Falls South," Jennifer Hunter,
Maclean's, July 5, 1999

CHAPTER SIX

1. *Weyerhaeuser Today*, May 1993

2. Bruce Zobel letter to Rex McCullough,
October 7, 1994

Bibliography

BOOKS

Hidy, Ralph W., Frank Earnest Hill, and Allan Nevins, *Timber and Men: The Weyerhaeuser Story*. New York: The MacMillan Company, 1963.

MacKay, Donald, *Empire of Wood: The MacMillan Bloedel Story*. Vancouver, B.C.: Douglas & McIntyre/ Seattle: University of Washington Press, 1982.

Prouty, Father Andrew Mason, *Logging with Steam in the Pacific Northwest: The Men, the Camps, and the Accidents, 1885–1918,* master's thesis. Seattle: University of Washington, 1973.

Staebler, George R., "Industrial forest research and forest science," *Forest Science: Evolution of Research Fields and Institutional Programs*. Durham, N.C.: Forest History Society (in press).

Twining, Charles E., *F. K. Weyerhaeuser: A Biography*. St. Paul: Minnesota Historical Society Press, 1997.

Twining, Charles E., *George S. Long: Timber Statesman*. Seattle: University of Washington Press, 1994.

Twining, Charles E., *Phil Weyerhaeuser: Lumberman*. Seattle: University of Washington Press, 1985.

ARTICLES

"An Ecologist in the Paper Industry," *Business Week*, March 6, 1971.

"Best of the S.O.B.s," *The Audubon Society Magazine*, September 1974.

"The Giant Falls South," *Maclean's*, July 5, 1999.

Historical Statistics of the United States, Colonial Times to 1970, Bicentennial Edition. Washington, D.C.: U.S. Bureau of the Census, 1975.

"I Think That I Shall Never See…," *Forbes*, July 15, 1974.

"Lost in the Woods," *Forbes*, October 16, 1989.

"Mars Mission," *Air & Space* magazine, October/November 1993.

"Missing the Forest for the Trees?" *Forbes*, September 15, 1975.

"The New Growth at Weyerhaeuser," *Business Week*, June 19, 1995.

"Old Boy, Did You Get Enough of Pie? A Social History of Food in Logging Camps," *Journal of Forest History*, Vol. 23, No. 4, October 1979.

A Partnership in Conservation: The Weyerhaeuser-EDF Management Plan for the Parker Tract, the Last Remnant of the East Dismal Swamp. Raleigh: Environmental Defense Fund, 1997.

Puget Sound Business Journal, South Sound/ Pierce County Edition, December 3, 1990; December 23, 1994.

"Rip Van Weyerhaeuser," *Forbes*, October 28, 1991.

The Roanoke Beacon, special supplement on the 25th anniversary of Weyerhaeuser in North Carolina, Roanoke, North Carolina, 1982.

Rough and Ready Loggers. Santa Fe: John Muir Publications, 1994.

"Swinging the Axe," *Maclean's*, February 16, 1998.

Transcript of the Senate Select Committee on Reforestation Hearings, 1922.

"The Tree No Longer Dominates," *Forbes*, December 2, 1985.

"Weyerhaeuser Gets Set for the 21st Century," *Fortune*, April 1977.

"Weyerhaeuser Picks Rogel as New CEO," *Wall Street Journal*, November 18, 1997.

"Weyerhaeuser Timber: Out of the Woods," *Fortune*, September 1959.

"What Worries Weyerhaeuser," *Eugene Register-Guard*, November 12, 1972.

"Why Weyerhaeuser's Prospects Look Bright," *Barron's*, October 25, 1993.

"With a Vengeance," *Canadian Business*, April 10, 1998.

"The Wobbly Horrors: Pacific Northwest Lumbermen and The Industrial Workers of the World, 1917–1918," *Labor History*, Vol. 24, Summer 1983.

"Women in Early Logging Camps: A Personal Reminiscence," *Journal of Forest History*, July 1975.

WEYERHAEUSER FAMILY PRIVATE PUBLICATIONS

Kohlmeyer, Fred W., *Frederick Weyerhaeuser: A Pen Portrait*, 1960.

Weyerhaeuser, Louise L., *Frederick Weyerhaeuser: Pioneer Lumberman*, Minneapolis, 1940.

WEYERHAEUSER COMPANY PUBLICATIONS AND MATERIALS IN THE WEYERHAEUSER ARCHIVES COLLECTION

Anderson, Steven, "The Changing Relationship Between Forest Industry and the American Public," January 31, 1998.

Jones, Alden H., *From Jamestown to Coffin Rock: A History of Weyerhaeuser Operations in Southwest Washington*. Weyerhaeuser Company, Tacoma, 1974.

McEwen, John M., *In the Chips: A History of Weyerhaeuser Company's Pulp and Paper Business*, Tacoma, 1978.

O'Rourke, Carroll, *History of Weyerhaeuser Advertising, 1914 to 1988*, July 19, 1990.

Smyth, Arthur V., *Weyerhaeuser in Washington, 1970–1984*, Tacoma, circa 1984.

A Celebration for Generations to Come: Clemons Tree Farm 50 Year Anniversary, Tacoma, 1990.

Commitment to Community: The Story of the Weyerhaeuser Company Foundation, Tacoma, 1989.

Connection newsletter, September 1996; August 1997; January 1998.

Customer Satisfaction newsletter, December 1988.

Environmental Stewardship, Tacoma: first edition 1990, second edition 1991, third edition 1993.

Gallery of Executive Officers, Tacoma, 1975.

Innovations and Trees: Weyerhaeuser, 1900–1975, Tacoma, 1975.

Men, Mills and Timber: Fifty Years of Progress in the Forest Industry, Tacoma, circa 1950.

Of Trees and Men: The Story of the Weyerhaeuser Companies, Tacoma, circa 1952.

Quality Works newsletter, Third Quarter 1996.

Westwood Shipping Lines: A Decade of Operation, a Century of Tradition, Tacoma, 1992.

Weyerhaeuser Bulletin No. 1994, June 24, 1999.

Weyerhaeuser Canada, Ltd.: A History, Vancouver, 1991.

Weyerhaeuser Company: A History of People, Land and Growth, Eastern Oregon Region, Klamath Falls, 1979.

Weyerhaeuser Company History, Tacoma, 1974.

Weyerhaeuser Magazine, August 1957; August 1959; September 1959; October 1959; February 1964, September 1964.

Weyerhaeuser Today, February 1992; March 1993; May 1993; February 1994; May 1996; December 1996.

Weyerhaeuser World, Tacoma, January 1970; May 1970; October 1970.

Where the Future Grows: A History of Weyerhaeuser Company, Tacoma, 1989.

Other monographs, publications, and company documents in the Weyerhaeuser Archives Collection.

Letters and documents in the personal collection of Joe Hughes, Weyerhaeuser Environmental Forester, New Bern, North Carolina.

PERSONAL INTERVIEWS—WEYERHAEUSER CURRENT AND FORMER EMPLOYEES, OFFICERS, AND DIRECTORS

Allen, J. R. "Junior," interview by the author, Dierks, Arkansas, March 31, 1998.

Allen, Jimmy, interview by the author, Dierks, Arkansas, March 31, 1998.

Allen, Marion, interview by the author, New Bern, North Carolina, April 2, 1998.

Andrews, Don, telephone interview by the author, May 19, 1998.

Anger, Rodger, interview by the author, New Bern, North Carolina, April 3, 1998.

Ashbrooks, Roger, interview by the author, Dierks, Arkansas, March 31, 1998.

Ayers, Tommie, interview by the author, Dierks, Arkansas, March 31, 1998.

Bickford, Mike, interview by the author, Federal Way, Washington, May 7, 1998.

Bingham, Charley, interview by the author and publisher, Fox Island, Washington, May 6, 1998.

Boyd, Billy, interview by the author, New Bern, North Carolina, April 2, 1998.

Boyd, Conor, interview by the author for *Weyerhaeuser Today,* Autumn 1997.

Brown, Curtis, interview by the author, New Bern, North Carolina, April 2, 1998.

Carpenter, Chuck, interview by the author, Federal Way, Washington, November 24, 1998.

Ciupitu, Regina, interview by the author, Hot Springs, Arkansas, April 1, 1998.

Collett, Jim, interview by the author, Bellevue, Washington, May 26, 1998.

Corbin, Bill, interview by the author, Federal Way, Washington, May 20, 1998.

Creighton, John W. "Jack," interview by Michael J. Parks, Federal Way, Washington, June 18, 1998; July 8, 1998.

Crossman, Liz, interview by the author, Federal Way, Washington, March 27, 1998.

Dale, Don, interview by the author, DeQueen, Arkansas, March 30, 1998.

Dowdy, Martha, interview by the author, Dierks, Arkansas, March 31, 1998.

Driscoll, John, interview by the author, Federal Way, Washington, December 2, 1998.

Elkin, Dave, interview by the author, DeQueen, Arkansas, March 30, 1998.

Franklin, Bill, interview by the author for *Weyerhaeuser Today,* Summer 1997; interview by the publisher, Seattle, Washington, September 21, 1998.

Freeman, Bobby, interview by the author, Mountain Pine, Arkansas, March 30, 1998.

Garrett, Michael, interview by the author,
New Bern, North Carolina, April 2, 1998.

Gozon, Dick, interview by the author and
publisher, Federal Way, Washington, May 15, 1998.

Henson, George, interview by the author,
Federal Way, Washington, May 29, 1998.

Hickman, Bonny, interview by Michele Komen,
Hot Springs, Arkansas, April 3, 1998.

Hill, Steve, interview by the author,
Federal Way, Washington, May 21, 1998.

Hogans, Mack, interview by the author and
publisher, Federal Way, Washington, May 13, 1998.

Holt, Sam, interview by the author,
New Bern, North Carolina, April 2, 1998.

Hughes, Joe, telephone interview by the author,
April 28, 1998.

Hunter, Rhonda, interview by Michele Komen,
DeQueen, Arkansas, April 3, 1998.

Irby, Mardy, interview by the author,
New Bern, North Carolina, April 2, 1998.

Janes, Herschel, interview by the author,
Dierks, Arkansas, March 31, 1998.

Jessup, Carl, interview by the author,
New Bern, North Carolina, April 3, 1998.

Jethro, Paul, telephone interview by the author,
November 17, 1998.

Johnson, Merlin, telephone interview by the author,
May 19, 1998.

Johnson, Norm, interview by the author,
Federal Way, Washington, April 17, 1998.

Kay, Paul, interview by the author, Federal Way,
Washington, November 16, 1998.

Leupold, Phil, telephone interview by the author,
September 1998.

Luthy, Tom, interview by the author and publisher,
Federal Way, Washington, May 28, 1998.

MacHaffie, Bruce, telephone interview by the
author, August 1998.

Mannigel, Jerry, telephone interview by the author,
September 1998.

Marshall, Scott, interview by the author,
Federal Way, Washington, March 12, 1998.

McCullough, Rex, interview by the author,
Federal Way, Washington, April 6, 1998.

Meadowcroft, Howie, interview by the author and
publisher, Tacoma, Washington, May 6, 1998.

Melchiors, Tony, interview by the author,
DeQueen, Arkansas, March 30, 1998.

Mendizabal, Frank, interview by the author,
Federal Way, Washington, September 8, 1998.

Miller, Doug, interview by the author,
Dierks, Arkansas, March 31, 1998.

Morgan, Harry Jr., interview by the author,
Tacoma, Washington, October 21, 1998.

Muise, Herb, interview by the author,
Federal Way, Washington, March 23, 1998.

Mumper, David, interview by the author,
Tacoma, Washington, September 25, 1998.

Nelson, Ted, interview by the author,
Federal Way, Washington, October 29, 1998.

Ragland, Jerry, interview by Michele Komen,
DeQueen, Arkansas, April 3, 1998.

Rogel, Steven R., interview by Michael J. Parks,
Federal Way, Washington, June 11, 1998;
July 8, 1998.

Ruckelshaus, William D., interview by the author
and publisher, Seattle, Washington,
December 4, 1998.

Rush, Don, interview by the author,
Federal Way, Washington, November 2, 1998.

Snyder, Bill, interview by the author, Dierks, Arkansas, March 31, 1998.

Sordi, Dino, telephone interview by the author, May 19, 1998.

Stamps, Jeff, interview by Michele Komen, Hot Springs, Arkansas, April 3, 1998.

Still, David, interview by the author and publisher, Federal Way, Washington, May 28, 1998.

Stivers, Bill, interview by the author, Federal Way, Washington, June 3, 1998.

Travis, Jim, interview by the author, New Bern, North Carolina, April 2, 1998.

Waters, Marvin, interview by the author, New Bern, North Carolina, April 2, 1998.

Weyerhaeuser, George H., interview by Michael J. Parks, Federal Way, Washington, August 4, 1987; June 8, 1998; July 2, 1998; July 8, 1998.

Weyerhaeuser, George H. Jr., interview by the author and publisher, Federal Way, Washington, May 18, 1998.

White, Kenny, interview by Michele Komen, DeQueen, Arkansas, April 3, 1998.

Wilkinson, John, telephone interview by the author, May 15, 1998.

Winward, Herb, interview by the author, Federal Way, Washington, December 2, 1998.

Wolff, Jack, interview by the author, Federal Way, Washington, November 3, 1998.

Wooten, Gil, telephone interview by the author, May 21, 1998.

Zagar, John, interview by the author, Federal Way, Washington, May 27, 1998.

PERSONAL INTERVIEWS—OTHERS

Anderson, Steve, executive director, Forest History Society, interview by the author, Durham, North Carolina, April 3, 1998.

Blayeloch, Janine, director of the Western Land Exchange Project, telephone interview by the author, September 1998.

Dillon, C. A. "Chip" III, analyst, Salomon Smith Barney, telephone interview by the author, September 1998.

Hay-Roe, Ross, founder of *Paper Tree Letter* (Miller Freeman: San Francisco), interview by Kevin Gudridge for *Marple's Business Newsletter*, July 21, 1999.

Markham, Dan'l, director of development, Willapa Alliance, telephone interview by the author, September 1998.

McAuley, Kathryn, analyst, Brown Brothers Harriman, telephone interview by the author, September 17, 1998.

McGehee, David, executive vice president, Mac Papers, telephone interview by the author, September 1998.

Orndorff, Bill, director of materials management, Perry Judd's, Inc., telephone interview by the author, September 1998.

Preyer, Jane, executive director, Environmental Defense Fund, interview by the author, Raleigh, North Carolina, April 1, 1998.

Raines, Charlie, director, Cascade Checkerboard Project, Sierra Club, telephone interview with the author, September 24, 1998.

Renner, Greg, marketing manager, Trusjoist MacMillan, telephone interview by the author, September 2, 1998.

Ryan, Dede, director of corporate communications, Trusjoist MacMillan, telephone interview by the author, August 31, 1998.

Directors and Terms

From January 18, 1900, to January 2000

NAME	*Elected*	*Served to*
Arthur F. Albertson★	January 18, 1900	June 21, 1900
William M. Allen	May 19, 1964	April 15, 1971
Robert O. Anderson	February 1, 1978	April 20, 1989
J. A. Auchter	May 22, 1962	May 18, 1965
F. S. Bell	June 29, 1910	March 13, 1938
Laird Bell	May 31, 1934	May 15, 1961
Carleton Blunt	May 18, 1953	April 15, 1976
William Carson★	January 18, 1900	July 5, 1932
A. W. Clapp	May 28, 1931	October 5, 1946
E. P. Clapp	June 16, 1921	May 30, 1946
Norton Clapp	May 30, 1946	April 15, 1976
William H. Clapp	October 13, 1981	April 15, 1997
Edmond M. Cook	May 26, 1949	April 11, 1968
John W. Creighton Jr.	April 21, 1988	April 22, 1998
George C. Crosby	November 20, 1957	October 23, 1963
E. W. Davis	May 27, 1947	May 20, 1953
Frederick C. A. Denkmann★	January 18, 1900	February 11, 1929
W. John Driscoll★★	August 14, 1979	
O. D. Fisher	May 26, 1949	May 15, 1961
Donald C. Frisbee	December 13, 1983	April 16, 1996
Booth Gardner	April 15, 1976	June 12, 1981
Richard F. Haskayne★★★		
John H. Hauberg	August 6, 1958	April 20, 1989
Philip M. Hawley★★	April 20, 1989	
Edmund Hayes	June 27, 1938	May 18, 1965
Harold J. Haynes	July 15, 1981	December 14, 1982
	June 11, 1985	April 16, 1992
Robert J. Herbold★★	October 14, 1999	
Robert S. Ingersoll	August 17, 1976	April 17, 1986
C. H. Ingram★	January 18, 1900	March 17, 1906
Charles H. Ingram	May 27, 1947	May 21, 1963
E. Bronson Ingram	April 13, 1967	April 30, 1995
Martha R. Ingram★★	October 11, 1995	
Herbert H. Irvine	June 19, 1902	February 26, 1947
Thomas Irvine★	January 18, 1900	June 19, 1902
Grant Keehn	May 19, 1964	May 18, 1965
Herbert M. Kieckhefer	April 30, 1957	May 18, 1965
John I. Kieckhefer★★	April 19, 1990	
Robert H. Kieckhefer	April 30, 1957	April 19, 1990
William H. Laird★	January 18, 1900	February 4, 1910
Artemus Lamb★	January 18, 1900	April 23, 1901
Lafayette Lamb	June 20, 1901	June 18, 1914

Leaders

From February 9, 1900, to January 2000

PRESIDENT	*Elected*	*Served to*
Frederick Weyerhaeuser	February 9, 1900	April 4, 1914
John P. Weyerhaeuser	June 18, 1914	May 31, 1928
F. S. Bell	May 31, 1928	May 31, 1934
F. E. Weyerhaeuser	May 31, 1934	October 18, 1945
Herbert H. Irvine	May 28, 1946	February 26, 1947
J. P. "Phil" Weyerhaeuser Jr.★	May 27, 1947	December 8, 1956
F. K. Weyerhaeuser	December 11, 1956	February 1, 1960
Norton Clapp	February 1, 1960	April 14, 1966
George H. Weyerhaeuser	April 14, 1966	April 21, 1988
John W. Creighton Jr.	April 21, 1988	December 1, 1997
Steven R. Rogel	December 1, 1997	

CHAIRMAN OF THE BOARD		
F. S. Bell	May 31, 1934	March 13, 1938
Laird Bell	May 17, 1947	March 7, 1955
F. K. Weyerhaeuser	March 7, 1955	March 8, 1957
Norton Clapp	March 8, 1957	February 1, 1960
F. K. Weyerhaeuser	February 1, 1960	April 14, 1966
Norton Clapp	April 14, 1966	April 15, 1976
Robert B. Wilson	April 15, 1976	April 21, 1988
George H. Weyerhaeuser	April 21, 1988	April 20, 1999
Steven R. Rogel	April 20, 1999	

GENERAL MANAGER		
George S. Long★★	June 29, 1910	April 29, 1915
George S. Long	April 29, 1915	May 30, 1929
F. R. Titcomb	May 30, 1929	September 29, 1936
Charles H. Ingram	September 29, 1936	December 11, 1956

★*Was executive vice president 1933-1947*

★★*After April 29, 1915, the office of general manager was a bylaw office.*

Significant Events

1900 Frederick Weyerhaeuser and fellow investors acquired 900,000 acres of Western Washington forestland from Northern Pacific Railway Company for $5.4 million on January 3, 1900

Weyerhaeuser Timber Company incorporated on January 18, 1900, with initial capital of $6 million

Weyerhaeuser Timber Company office opened in Tacoma, Washington

1901 Weyerhaeuser increased its capital stock to $8 million

1902 Weyerhaeuser acquired Bell-Nelson, which became Mill A in Everett, Washington

Yacolt Burn destroyed 23 square miles of Weyerhaeuser timberland in southwestern Washington

First purchase of Oregon forestland occurred

Weyerhaeuser increased its capital stock to $10 million

1903 Yacolt salvage logging began

1905 Weyerhaeuser increased its capital stock to $12.5 million

First purchase of pine forests in Oregon and Northern California

First cooperative study of sustainable forestry completed

1906 San Francisco earthquake and fire created great demand for Pacific Northwest lumber

1908 Weyerhaeuser developed an employee health plan, likely the first in the forest products industry

Washington Forest Fire Association established

1911 The Tacoma Building, Weyerhaeuser's corporate headquarters, opened in Tacoma

1914 Snoqualmie Falls Lumber Company established by the Weyerhaeuser Timber Company and partners

Panama Canal opened

1915 Mill B, first mill built by Weyerhaeuser and the nation's first all-electric sawmill, opened in Everett, Washington

Thompson Yards established as Weyerhaeuser's first Midwest and East retail distribution arm

1916 Weyerhaeuser Sales Company formed in St. Paul, Minnesota; was incorporated in 1919

1917 United States entered World War I

Thompson Yards grew to 120 retail lumber distribution yards

Land acquired for an eastern distribution center at Baltimore, Maryland

Snoqualmie Falls Lumber Company mill opened

Snoqualmie Falls mill began burning waste wood to generate steam and electricity

1918 Weyerhaeuser employees began working eight-hour (rather than 10-hour) days

World War I ended

1919 Clemons Logging Company acquired

1920 Thompson Yards grew to 193 retail lumber distribution centers

First national advertising campaign using the Weyerhaeuser Forest Products trademark began

1921 Wood Conversion Company organized to produce new products from waste wood

Postwar recession began

The Baltimore Yard, Weyerhaeuser's "Eastern Forest," opened

1922 Balsam wool (insulation) plant constructed by Wood Conversion Company

Weyerhaeuser donated 5,000 acres to the state of Washington for reforestation research

1923 Weyerhaeuser purchased its first World War I surplus steamships, the *Hanley* and the *Pomona*

The Klamath Falls, Oregon, mill site acquired

1924 Congress passed Clarke-McNary Act to encourage sustainable forestry

First full-time professional forester, Charles S. Chapman, hired

1925 Weyerhaeuser Logged Off Land Company organized

The Longview, Washington, mill site was acquired

1926 Second eastern distribution yard opened in Portsmouth, Rhode Island

1927 Newark, New Jersey, distribution yard opened

1928 4-Square® trademark introduced

Construction began on Longview and Klamath Falls sawmills

1929 Longview sawmills 1, 2, and 3 started operations

Klamath Falls sawmill began production

White River Lumber Company, originally formed in 1897, became affiliated with Weyerhaeuser

Snoqualmie Falls Lumber Company Mill 2 closed by fire

The stock market crashed and the Great Depression began

1930 Company began box manufacturing at Klamath Falls

1931 Sulfite pulp production began at Longview

Willapa Harbor Lumber Mills organized

Weyerhaeuser's stock split 6 shares for 1

1933 Weyerhaeuser Steamship Company established

Weyerhaeuser pulp research and development laboratory opened in Longview

Everett Mill A closed, its site later used to construct the Everett pulp mill

1934 Company began Pres-to-log® production at Longview

First sustained yield plan developed

Philadelphia Wholesale Yard opened

Brooklyn Wholesale Yard opened

1936 Weyerhaeuser Logged Off Land Company liquidated, Reforestation and Land Department formed

Everett sulfite pulp mill began production

1937 Sustainable forestry program announced

"Timber Is A CROP!" corporate advertising began

Weyerhaeuser's stock split 4 shares for 1

1938 First seedling nursery opened at Snoqualmie Falls, Washington

First company forest plantations established

1940 Selective logging practices began on Klamath Falls forestland

Washington Veneer Company acquired, marking the company's entrance into the plywood business

1941 Clemons Tree Farm, the nation's first certified tree farm, dedicated

United States entered World War II

1942 Forestry research department established

Weyerhaeuser steamships S. S. *Heffron* and S. S. *Potlatch* sunk by enemy action

Snoqualmie Falls Tree Farm certified

1944 Snoqualmie Falls Lumber converted from railroad to truck transportation of logs to mill

White River Tree Farm established

1945 World War II ended

Retirement plan to cover salaried employees began

1946 First diesel locomotives purchased

ENIAC, the world's first computer, was invented

1947 Production of Silvacon® made from tree bark began

Plywood production began at Longview

1948 Weyerhaeuser Timber Company Foundation established

Snoqualmie Falls Lumber Company and Ewauna Box Company dissolved into Weyerhaeuser Timber Company

Washington Veneer Company sold

Magnesium oxide pulp process began at Longview

Wood Conversion Company became a partially owned subsidiary

Weyerhaeuser Sales Company became a wholly owned subsidiary

1949 White River Lumber Company and Willapa Harbor Lumber Mills dissolved into Weyerhaeuser Timber Company

Company's first kraft pulp production began at Longview

Helicopter seeding started

Company began lumber, pulp, and container-board manufacturing at Springfield

1950 Weyerhaeuser's stock split 2 for 1 share

United States entered the Korean War

1951 Sawmill and export facilities opened at North Bend (Coos Bay), Oregon

Company contributed $1 million to Weyerhaeuser Timber Foundation

1952 First paperboard mill began operation at Longview

First wood fiber plant (Silvacel®) began production at Snoqualmie Falls

Plywood plant began production at Springfield

Klamath Falls hardboard plant construction began

1955 Weyerhaeuser's stock split 4 for 1 share

1956 First southern United States timberland acquired in Mississippi and Alabama

1957 Kieckhefer Container Company and Eddy Paper Corporation acquired; Weyerhaeuser entered packaging business

1958 Weyerhaeuser International, S.A., formed

1959 Weyerhaeuser Timber Company renamed Weyerhaeuser Company

Weyerhaeuser Sales Company merged into Weyerhaeuser

Retail lumberyards of the original Thompson Yards sold

1960 Rilco Laminated Products and Roddis Plywood acquired, marking Weyerhaeuser's first operations in Canada

1961 First harvest of second-growth forestland in Pacific Northwest

Weyerhaeuser acquired Hamilton Paper Company to enter fine paper business

Kunst Im Druck-Obpacher A.G. acquired, with folded packaging and milk carton plants in Germany, Venezuela, and Belgium

Springfield pulp mill won the Industrial Air and Water Protection Award from the Pacific Northwest Pollution Control Association

1962 The Columbus Day storm downed 83,000 acres of high-volume forestland

Specialty paper producer Crocker, Burbank & Company acquired

1963 Weyerhaeuser listed on the New York and Pacific Stock Exchanges

Sales office opened in Tokyo, Japan

Weyerhaeuser's container manufacturing operations expanded with its 50 percent acquisition of Cajas y Empaques de Guatemala, S.A.

1964 First European sales office opened in Paris, France

Weyerhaeuser acquired Dropsy, S.A., container plants in France and South Africa

Weyerhaeuser entered joint venture to build pulp mill at Kamloops, British Columbia

1965 Clean Air Act enacted

1966 Weyerhaeuser acquired 750,000 acres of hardwood forests in Malaysia and the Philippine Republic

1967 High Yield Forestry program announced

First Weyerhaeuser sawmill in southern United States opened at Philadelphia, Mississippi

1968 Weyerhaeuser acquired container manufacturers Papeteries du Forez (France) and Contonneries de Grand Bigard, NV (Belgium), and Whitman Lumber Company (Ontario, Canada)

Gold Medal for water pollution control awarded by the National Sports Foundation to Kamloops, British Columbia, and Cosmopolis, Washington, mills

Springfield mill won second award for air and water pollution control from the Pacific Northwest Pollution Control Association

1969 Weyerhaeuser entered commercial real estate development business

Dierks Forests, Inc., acquired, adding 1.8 million acres of forestland in Arkansas and Oklahoma to Weyerhaeuser's southern United States holdings

Weyerhaeuser Real Estate Company (WRECO) formed

Kamloops pulp mill began production

Company acquired Blue River Sawmills, Ltd., in Kamloops and Merritt, British Columbia

Weyerhaeuser acquired cutting rights on 250,000 acres in Indonesia

Weyerhaeuser acquired Par-West Financial, Pardee Construction Company, and Quadrant Corporation

Weyerhaeuser's stock split 2 for 1 share

The second sawmill and pulp mill at New Bern, North Carolina, started up

1970 The first Earth Day celebrated

Clean Air Act Amendment added

Weyerhaeuser acquired Centennial Homes, Inc., in Dallas, Texas

Weyerhaeuser entered disposable diaper business

1971 Weyerhaeuser corporate headquarters moved from Tacoma to Federal Way, Washington

Weyerhaeuser Canada, Ltd., formed

Production began at Valliant, Oklahoma, containerboard mill, the largest of its type in the world

Business Week magazine gave Weyerhaeuser one of five national Business Citizenship Awards for efforts to improve the environment

Federal government instigated wage and price controls

Weyerhaeuser's Asian forestlands expanded to 2 million acres

Company received a total of 83 awards for safety performance during 1971

1972 Clean Water Act enacted

Weyerhaeuser Real Estate Company acquired the Florida residential builder Babcock Company

Business relations with the People's Republic of China began at Guangzhou (Canton) Trade Fair

Weyerhaeuser Canada built a new mill in Vavenby, British Columbia

1973 "The Tree Growing Company" advertisement campaign began

Endangered Species Act enacted

Weyerhaeuser's stock split 2 for 1 share

World oil embargo greatly increased the cost of petroleum fuels, 1,000 percent for crude oil, 670 percent for diesel, which greatly increased the cost of transportation

1974 Weyerhaeuser entered paper recycling business

1975 Weyerhaeuser International established Far East region headquarters in Hong Kong

Tropical Forestry Research Center opened in Indonesia

Weyerhaeuser acquired Combustion Power Company for its cogeneration and municipal waste technology

Fine paper facilities at Fitchburg, Massachusetts, and White Pigeon, Michigan, divested

Veneer and panel plants in Pennsylvania, Virginia, and Arkansas acquired from Evans Products

1976 North Pacific Paper Corporation (NORPAC), a joint venture between Weyerhaeuser and Jujo Paper (later renamed Nippon Paper Industries), formed

Weyerhaeuser Business Conduct Committee established

The last large-log mill constructed at Longview

Weyerhaeuser contributed 11,000 acres for Great Dismal Swamp wildlife refuge in North Carolina

Original lumber mill in Longview demolished

1977 Sold and turned back mills and cutting rights in Far East Asia

1978 Weyerhaeuser Technology Center opened

1979 NORPAC newsprint mill opened in Longview

1980 On May 18, Mount St. Helens erupted and destroyed 68,000 acres of Weyerhaeuser forestland

Weyerhaeuser shipping operations became known as Westwood Shipping Lines

Short-term interest rates exceeded 20 percent and mortgage rates climbed above 16 percent

Weyerhaeuser sold specialty paper mills in Pennsylvania and Michigan

1981 First high-technology, high-speed small-log mill opened at Raymond, Washington

Weyerhaeuser became the largest United States manufacturer of private-label disposable diapers

1982 Company acquired Wright Nurseries of Cairo, California

Company's first oriented strand board (OSB) plant opened at Grayling, Michigan, to produce Structurwood®

State-of-the-art Columbus, Mississippi, pulp and paper complex opened

1983 Salvage of Mount St. Helens forestland completed

Shemin Nurseries acquired

Weyerhaeuser acquired 80 percent interest in Great Northern Insured Annuity Corporation (GNA)

1984 Weyerhaeuser Mortgage Company acquired Mason-McDuffie Mortgage Company

Microboard® plant opened at Moncure, North Carolina, to produce wood-fiber components for the furniture industry

Weyerhaeuser entered hydroponic food business with acquisition of Waterfield Farms greenhouse

Weyerhaeuser opened office in Beijing, China

1985 Through acquisitions, Weyerhaeuser became the nation's largest nursery stock supplier

Financial services expanded with the acquisition of Republic Federal Savings and Loan

Businesses grouped in three organizations: Weyerhaeuser Forest Products Company, Weyerhaeuser Paper Company, and Weyerhaeuser Real Estate Company and Diversified

1986 Weyerhaeuser planted its two-billionth seedling, commemorating the completion of an 18-million-seedling reforestation effort on land near Mount St. Helens

Prince Albert pulp mill and timber licenses acquired in Saskatchewan, Canada

Weyerhaeuser became the first United States forest products company to be listed on the Tokyo Stock Exchange

1987 Development of Washington State's Timber, Fish and Wildlife Agreement began

Interest acquired in Pelican Spruce Mills, Ltd.—which included two OSB mills, three sawmills, and a building materials distribution system—of Edmonton, Alberta

1988 Hydroponic food and salmon ranching enterprises sold

Weyerhaeuser's stock split 3 for 2 shares

1989 Company began major restructuring, a process of refocusing on its core business

NORPAC expanded to include de-inking facility

Weyerhaeuser's gypsum, milk carton, and hardwood paneling businesses and Weyerhaeuser Australia, Ltd., sold

1990 Continued divestments included wholesale nursery and garden supply businesses and home construction firms

1991 Springfield and Klamath Falls lumber mills closure announced

Recycling centers opened in Los Angeles, California; Wichita, Kansas; Denver, Colorado; and Portland, Oregon

1992 Company values documented

Weyerhaeuser vision statement "The Best Forest Products Company in the World" created

Everett mill closure announced

Company mills were among the first on the continent to receive ISO 9000 series quality registration

$500 million Plymouth, North Carolina, modernization began

Diaper business sold through public offering

Sale of GNA announced

Two pulp mills, three sawmills, and Georgia forestland acquired from Procter & Gamble

Weyerhaeuser acquired OSB mill at Slave Lake, Alberta

Republic Federal Savings & Loan Association dissolved

1993 The Clinton Timber Plan restricted logging in federal forests in Pacific Northwest

$400 million Longview mill modernization began

Recycling facilities expanded at Springfield and Valliant containerboard mills

Columbus pulp and paper mill was first company operation to receive OSHA's STAR award for its on-the-job safety record

Winchester Homes in Virginia and Maryland won the first National Housing Quality Award

1994 Weyerhaeuser adopted uniform Forestry Resource Goals for all of its U.S. forestland

Weyerhaeuser submitted Oregon's first habitat conservation plan for the northern spotted owl

Weyerhaeuser Real Estate sold Scarborough Corporation in New Jersey, Scarborough Constructors in Florida, and Westminster Homes in North Carolina

1995 World Timberfund, a joint venture, formed to invest in Southern Hemisphere forestlands

Weyerhaeuser ranked number 1 in United States for responsibility to community and the environment by *Fortune* magazine

Performance Share Plan extended to virtually all Weyerhaeuser employees

Weyerhaeuser acquired 10 container plants from Westvaco

Nine recycling collection centers added

Wild Turkey Partnership Agreement signed

1996 Weyerhaeuser sold its Oregon pine forestland, 600,000 acres near Klamath Falls

Company acquired two sawmills and additional southern forestland in Mississippi and Louisiana from Cavenham Forest Industries

Weyerhaeuser Forestlands International formed a partnership with UBS Resource Investments International to purchase and manage Southern Hemisphere forestland

Weyerhaeuser Mortgage Company sold

Sutton, West Virginia, OSB mill started up

Cedar River Paper Company, a containerboard mill using exclusively recycled fiber, opened in Iowa

1997 Flint River, Georgia, mill became first forest products facility accepted into the U.S. Environmental Protection Agency's XL Program

Shemin Nurseries and Weyerhaeuser Mortgage Company sold

Weyerhaeuser's forestlands expanded to include managed forest and new plantations in New Zealand and Uruguay

Weyerhaeuser and the Environmental Defense Fund announced a joint conservation plan for managing the Parker Tract in the East Dismal Swamp in North Carolina

1998 Weyerhaeuser's Canadian presence expanded into Ontario with the acquisition of two sawmills, a fine paper mill, and timber licenses from Bowater at Dryden, Ontario

Production began at a Shanghai, China, container plant built by Weyerhaeuser in a joint venture with Sweden's SCA Packaging

New Bern pulp mill started up the world's first commercial application of gasification technology

1999 Weyerhaeuser acquired one of Canada's largest forest products companies, MacMillan Bloedel

Weyerhaeuser box plant opened in Mexico

SCA Weyerhaeuser packaging plant opened in Wuhan, China

2000 First commercial harvest of High Yield Forestry-grown pine on southern U.S. forestlands

Acknowledgments

When Weyerhaeuser first began planning the celebration for its 100th anniversary, it was decided early in the process to have a written chronicle of the company's history. In the course of reviewing the company's already well-documented legacy and developing editorial objectives for a history book, a clear pattern emerged. Weyerhaeuser's strong values, passed from one generation to the next, were at the core of its success. So rather than write the book from a traditional year-to-year perspective, it was determined that the story of Weyerhaeuser would be told through its values: what they are, where they came from, how they work, and how they will likely influence the destiny of the company.

This book, like the beginnings of Weyerhaeuser, was truly a collaborative effort. The company's Centennial Team—Michele Komen, Vicky Howry, and Lee Bjorklund—developed the editorial objectives and creative approach along with publisher Barry Provorse, who also provided perspective, guidance, and his exceptional expertise.

Author Joni Sensel drew on her years of experience working for Weyerhaeuser, first as an employee and later as a supplier. She dug deep into company archives, conducted myriad interviews, and plowed through hundreds of publications (including the 700-plus pages of *Timber and Men*) to weave together the rich textures of Weyerhaeuser's history.

Chuck Twining, author of several books about past Weyerhaeuser leaders, including Phil Weyerhaeuser, Frederick K. Weyerhaeuser, and George S. Long, served as consulting historian and shared his contagious enthusiasm with and greatly facilitated research for the author.

Each of the company's senior executives, including its recently retired chairman George Weyerhaeuser; its retired president and chief executive officer Jack Creighton; and its current chairman, chief executive officer, and president, Steve Rogel, gave his support, time, recollections, and observations to this work. George Weyerhaeuser's unique contribution to the project—with his 50 years of service to the company, superb memory, and attention to detail—was especially appreciated.

Weyerhaeuser archivists Pauline Larson and Megan Moholt greatly assisted efforts to ferret out historical gems and document even the most obscure facts used in this book. They read text, made corrections, and offered suggestions. Then, from deep in the vast company archives, they gathered a selection of meaningful photographs to illustrate the text.

Corporate librarians Young Hong and Jerry Eckrom assisted in procuring current documents and selecting contemporary photographs for use in the book. Weyerhaeuser photographers Dave Putnam and Gary Darby captured many of these exceptional images.

Centennial manager Michele Komen, the Weyerhaeuser editor for the book, developed and managed the internal review and distribution processes, consolidated and integrated input and suggestions, and served as liaison with the publisher.

Dozens of current and retired Weyerhaeuser employees, from production crew members to retired senior officers, freely shared heartfelt comments and anecdotes with the author, and provided considerable insight into the spirit of the company. In addition, a large number of people (noted below) reviewed the text, providing suggestions and ensuring accuracy in their areas of expertise.

The book's external editorial team was led by publisher Barry Provorse and impeccably managed by Carolyn Margon. Story editor Don Graydon made the text flow seamlessly with a single voice, and copy editor Judy Gouldthorpe clarified even the most obscure parts of many drafts.

Designer Paul Langland created a visually powerful and exciting book with his careful choice of typefaces and placement of photographs near the stories they illustrated.

It is through the combined efforts of these and the people listed below that *Traditions Through the Trees* has become the story of Weyerhaeuser's history and values. These values, which can be traced to the company's founders, have directed its success throughout the first 100 years. And as George Weyerhaeuser observed, "Our history has proven the worth of our company's uncommonly strong values, and they provide the promise of equal or greater successes during Weyerhaeuser's next 100 years."

In addition to the above-mentioned people, special thanks are extended to the many people who over the last 100 years faithfully documented Weyerhaeuser's activities in its many publications and to the following individuals and organizations for their myriad contributions to the publication of this book.

Weyerhaeuser employees have contributed to the company's legacy since 1900. Shown at Camp No. 1 in 1912 are some of the company's pioneer employees who worked for a Weyerhaeuser subsidiary, Cherry Valley Timber Company, and harvested forests near the Snoqualmie River in northern King County, Washington.

J. R. "Junior" Allen
Jimmy Allen
Marion Allen
Bruce Amundson
Steve Anderson
Don Andrews
Rodger Anger
Roger Ashbrooks
Tommie Ayers
Bruce Beckett
Dan Berglund
Mike Bickford
Charley Bingham
Cheri Bischel
Liz Bishop
Janine Blayeloch
Billy Boyd
Conor Boyd
Curtis Brown
Bill Cafferata
Chuck Carpenter
Eileen Cavanagh
Regina Ciupitu
Linda Coady
David Coburn
Jim Collett
Bill Corbin
Liz Crossman
Paul Dahl
Don Dale
C. A. "Chip" Dillon III
Martha Dowdy
John Driscoll
Kathy Edwards
Dave Elkin
Dick Erickson
Marc Finlayson
Bill Franklin
Bobby Freeman

Charlie Gadzik
Omar Gallardo
Michael Garrett
Dick Gozon
Graphic Arts Center
Jim Hanson
Rullie Harris
Kent Harrison
Leo Hassa
Ross Hay-Roe
George Henson
Bonny Hickman
Steve Hill
Mack Hogans
Sam Holt
Rhonda Hunter
Mardy Irby
Herschel Janes
Deb Jensen
Carl Jessup
Paul Jethro
Merlin Johnson
Norm Johnson
Joe Jughes
Paul Kay
Jim Keller
Pat King
Dewey Knight
Venessa Koehn
Russel Kolasa
George Kovich
Diane LaCasse
My Duyen Lam
Dave Larsen
Phil Leupold
Steve Lewis
Sally Lofquist
Tom Luthy
Roger Lyons
Bruce MacHaffie
Montye Male
Jerry Mannigel
Dan'l Markham

Scott Marshall
Kathryn McAuley
Rex McCullough
David McGehee
Jill McLain
John McMahon
Jim McPherson
Howie Meadowcroft
Jay Mehta
Tony Melchiors
Frank Mendizabal
Bob Meyer
Dave Miller
Doug Miller
Harry Morgan Jr.
Herb Muise
Dave Mumper
Carol Nelson
Dave Nelson
Ted Nelson
Marlene O'Byrne
Bill Orndorff
Mike Parks
Linda Parsons
Sally Penley
Dick Pierson
Lawrence Pillon
Deanna Powell
Jack Presson
Jane Preyer
Kert Quashie
Jerry Ragland
Charlie Raines
Greg Renner
The people at
    Weyerhaeuser
    Rothschild,
    Wisconsin

Bill Ruckelshaus
Don Rush
Dede Ryan
Jeanne Schaeffer
Seema Scholl
Jim Schott
Anne Shayler
Bill Snyder
Dino Sordi
Jeff Stamps
Pete Steen
Paula Stewart
David Still
Bill Stivers
Neal Sullins
Dick Taggart
Kate Tate
Nancy Thomas
Chapin Titcomb
Jim Travis
Ron Van Pool
Bill Von Brauchitsch
Don Walls
Marvin Waters
George Weyerhaeuser Jr.
Kenny White
Teresa Wiant
Sue Wieker
John Wilkinson
Penny Willet
Peter Winkler
Herb Winward
Jack Wolff
Gary Wong
Gil Wooten
Bob Wroblewski
Jimmy Wyatt
Don Young
Greg Yuckert
John Zagar

Index

Page numbers in *italics* indicate captions and/or photographs

F. S. Bell
President, 1928 – 1934
Chairman, 1934 – 1938

F. R. Titcomb
General Manager,
1929 – 1936

F. E. Weyerhaeuser
President,
1934 – 1945

Charles H. Ingram
General Manager,
1936 – 1956
Executive Vice President,
1956 – 1958

H. H. Irvine
President,
1946 – 1947

J. P. We
Preside
Execut
1933 –

1931 Weyerhaeuser entered
the pulp business

1937 "Timber Is A CROP!" campaign

1948 Weyerh
Company Fo

Company steamship, 1923

1933 Weyerhaeuser began
pollution control research

1933 Weyerhaeuser Steamship
Company incorporated

Weyerhaeuser Steamship Company, World War II

1949
comp

1949
contai

erhaeuser
first steamships

4 Charles S. "Chet" Chapman, first
-time forester, hired

1941 Clemons Tree
Farm dedicated

1942 Corporate forestry
research began

Band saw sharpening,

1925 Weyerhaeuser Logged Off Land
Company formed

1929 Klamath Falls mill opened

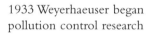

1928, 4-Square brand unveiled

1937 Sustained-yield forestry principles
adopted, applied to selected company lands

1947 Longview plywo
opened

on

1929 Longview, Washington,
Mills 1, 2, and 3 opened

1945 First employee
pension plan offered

land,

1930
The Great Depression

924
he Clarke-McNary Act

1929
Stock Market crash

1941
World War II

1946
ENIAC, the world's first c

▲
1930

▲
1940

WEYERHAEUSER TIME LINE 1900–2000

LEADERS

Frederick Weyerhaeuser
President, 1900 – 1914

George S. Long
Resident Agent,
1900 – 1910
General Manager,
1910 – 1929

John P. Weyerhaeuser
President, 1914 – 1928

MILESTONES

January 3, 1900, 900,000-acre Pacific
Northwest timberland purchase

January 18, 1900 Weyerhaeuser
Timber Company founded

1902 Bell–Nelson Mill acquired,
Everett, Washington

1902 First Oregon timberland purchase
at Coos Bay, Oregon

1911 The Tacoma Building, Weyerhaeuser's
headquarters, opened

Weyerhaeuser surveyors, 1913

Weyerhaeuse

1923 We
purchase

19
ful

1908 Weyerhaeuser Employee
Health Plan began

1917 Snoqualmie Falls
Lumber mill opened

Tacoma, Washington, headquarters, 1900

Everett Mill B

1921 Wood Convers
Company founded

1921 Baltimore, Ma
Yard opened

WORLD AND ENVIRONMENTAL EVENTS

1902
Yacolt Fire

1906
San Francisco Earthquake

1914
Panama Canal opened

1917
U. S. entered World War I

1900

1910

1920

John W. "Jack" Creighton Jr.
President, 1988 – 1997
Chief Executive, 1991 – 1997

Steven R. Rogel
President, 1997 –
Chief Executive, 1997 –
Chairman, 1999 –

1979 NORPAC newsprint mill opened

1992 Everett mill
closure announced

ɔn

erhaeuser entered the
cling business

1986 two billionth seedling
planted by Weyerhaeuser

H. R. MacMillan, MacMillan Bloedel

Mount St. Helens eruption damage, 1980

1992 Vision and Values formalized

1984 Weyerhaeuser opened an
office in Beijing, China

1999 MacMillan
Bloedel acquired

1978 Weyerhaeuser
Technology Center opened

1995 World Timberfund
formation announced

Growing
ign

1995 Performance
Share Plan created

founded

1981 Weyerhaeuser opened its
first high-tech small-log mill

2000 First harvest of
southern High Yield
forestlands

Recycling center, Kent, Washington

May 18, 1980
ɔecies Act   Mount St. Helens erupted

1993
The Clinton Timber Plan

1980

1990

2000

aeuser Jr.
947 – 1956
Vice President,
7

F. K. Weyerhaeuser
President, 1956 – 1960
Chairman, 1955 – 1957,
1960 – 1966

Norton Clapp
President, 1960 – 1966
Chairman, 1957 – 1960,
1966 – 1976

George H. Weyerhaeuser
President, 1966 – 1988
Chief Executive, 1966 – 1991
Chairman, 1988 – 1999

r Timber
tion established

1963 Weyerhaeuser Company listed
on the New York Stock Exchange

1971 Weyerhaeuser headquarters
opened in Federal Way, Washingt

gfield, Oregon,
pened

1961 Weyerhaeuser entered
fine paper business

1967 High Yield Forestry
principles adopted

1974 Wey
paper rec

pany began
oard manufacturing

1961 First western
second-growth harvest

1967 First southern sawmill acquired

Cruising southern timberlands, 1957

Dierks acquisition, 1960s

1957 Kieckhefer Container/Eddy
Paper Corporation acquired

1964 Weyerhaeuser opened
first office in Europe

0s

mill

1956 First southern timberland
purchase (Mississippi and Alabama)

1965 Kamloops mill opened in
British Columbia, Canada

1973 "The Tree
Company" camp

1959 Weyerhaeuser Timber Company
renamed Weyerhaeuser Company

1971 Weyerhaeuser Canada, Ltd.

1951 North Bend,
Oregon, mill opened

1963 Weyerhaeuser opened first sales
office in Tokyo, Japan

1969 Dierks Forests acquired

950
he Korean War

1965
Clean Air Act

1972
Clean Water Act

uter

1962
Columbus Day storm

1965
The Vietnam War

1970
First Earth Day

1973
Endangered S

0

▲
1960

▲
1970